Learning and teaching in social work education: Textbooks and frameworks on assessment

Beth R. Crisp, Mark R. Anderson, Joan Orme and
Pam Green Lister

First published in Great Britain in April 2005
by the Social Care Institute for Excellence

Written by Beth R. Crisp, Mark R. Anderson, Joan Orme and
Pam Green Lister (Glasgow School of Social Work, University
of Glasgow)

ISBN 1-904812-21-X

Produced by The Policy Press
Fourth Floor, Beacon House
Queen's Road
Bristol BS8 1QU
tel 0117 331 4054
fax 0117 331 4093
tpp-info@bristol.ac.uk
www.policypress.org.uk

**This report is available in print and online
www.scie.org.uk**

Social Care Institute for Excellence
Goldings House
2 Hay's Lane
London SE1 2HB
tel 020 7089 6840
fax 020 7089 6841
textphone 020 7089 6893
www.scie.org.uk

Executive summary

This review examined two types of publications from which readers might seek information about the assessment process, namely textbooks and assessment frameworks. Although often criticised for their lack of depth on the topics they cover, in terms of sales and readership, textbooks are often claimed to be highly influential in shaping the understanding of social work students and practitioners. However, increasingly over the past decade or so, assessment practice in the UK has involved the use of standardised frameworks such as the *Framework for the assessment of children in need and their families.*[1]

Both textbooks and assessment frameworks are widely read documents that have the potential to lead to significant changes in practice, but there are some significant differences between the two as well as considerable variation between documents of the same type. To some extent, it would seem that textbooks and assessment frameworks complement each other rather than one being a substitute for the other.

No single definition or conceptualisation of assessment was readily apparent in either the study on textbooks or the study on assessment frameworks, although the identification and management of risk emerged as a common purpose for assessment in the assessment frameworks. Moreover, a number of documents reviewed failed to indicate what the authors meant by the term 'assessment' per se. Absence of a definition seems more likely in documents that were aimed at a more advanced audience than beginning social work students or newly appointed unqualified workers. One of the differences between textbooks and assessment frameworks is that the former are more likely to include explicit discussion of theoretical underpinnings in relation to assessment, and the latter are more likely to include specific guidelines about how practice should be undertaken. However, numerous exceptions to such generalisations hold. For example, some frameworks provide as weighty a discussion on theoretical matters as many textbooks. Conversely, some textbooks provide detailed practice guidelines that can be adapted for use in several settings.

All of the frameworks examined, and 13 of the 16 textbooks, were written for audiences in the UK or particular countries therein. However, the extent to which these took account of current practice concerns varied considerably. Very few textbooks or assessment frameworks included content from service users or carers with regard to their perspective of being assessed or discussed issues in relation to conducting assessments with clients whose first language is other than English. Even among those documents developed for use in the UK, there was considerable variation in relation to the extent, if any, of any mention of anti-discriminatory/ anti-oppressive practice, legislation, and involvement of service users and carers in the assessment process. Mentions of these concerns were scant to non-existent in the textbooks produced overseas.

The explicitness of the evidence bases that underpinned writing on assessment also varied greatly. Two of the frameworks typologised all forms of evidence cited, and the reader could readily identify what type of evidence was being used to support particular guidelines. None of the textbooks systematically typologised evidence they cited in this way. While some textbooks explicitly discussed research findings, often the only way for the reader to gain insight into what form of evidence was included in citations was to go back to the original source material itself.

A final concern of this review was transferability of knowledge and there are a number of findings in relation to this. First, much of the guidance provided in the various frameworks is often applicable for assessing populations other than those for which they were originally envisaged, although it is left to the reader to apply these principles more broadly. Second, textbooks reflect the concerns of both the era and national setting in which they are written. Although textbooks written outside the UK and those written some years ago might make valuable contributions in relation to several issues associated with assessment, they are likely to need contextualising through supplementary readings which address the contemporary UK practice context. Third, differing legal systems within the UK can limit the transferability of information in textbooks and assessment frameworks between England, Wales, Scotland and Northern Ireland in relation to legal frameworks and legislation.

All of the documents examined for this review had some shortcomings in respect of (a) the adequacy with which they covered key content areas and/or (b) the inclusion of pedagogical devices to encourage. As the potential readership of information on assessment is, in the main, likely to be busy students or practitioners who do not have unlimited time for reading, it is important that what reading on assessment is recommended is most appropriate for a particular readership. While the findings pertained in this review are likely to be of most interest to those social work educators[2] who are deciding what books or frameworks they might use to promote learning about assessment to either students or practitioners, the approach taken for this review also provides a model for critiquing and selecting learning materials for social work education more generally. This involved identifying (a) how assessment was conceptualised, (b) theoretical and evidence bases, (c) current practice concerns and determining the adequacy of information provided in relation to these, and (d) pedagogical aids to enhance learning. This approach could readily be adapted for reviewing learning resources for other aspects of the social work curriculum, and also for learning materials produced for cognate disciplines such as the health sciences and education.

Taking the findings of this review further, we wish to conclude by making recommendations about textbooks and assessment frameworks for all readers as well as specific guidelines for social work educators and authors.

Recommendations for all readers

- Readers need to be aware that legislative, policy and practice contexts are not static, and should not assume that textbooks and assessment frameworks that have been published for some time are an accurate reflection of current practice.
- Readers need to be particularly aware that some textbooks, especially those published overseas, reflect rather different contexts for social work practice. On the other hand, such textbooks may offer useful insights, especially on topics poorly covered in local literature.
- Readers in the UK need to be aware that there will be some differences in legislation and organisation of practice between England, Wales, Scotland and Northern Ireland.
- Readers should not assume that they will develop expertise in assessment only by reading relevant textbooks and assessment frameworks. Attempting learning exercises contained in textbooks and assessment frameworks, discussion of concepts and practices in supervision, and

ultimately attempting to put the theory into practice, are all further steps in becoming a skilled practitioner.

Recommendations for social work educators

- It is unlikely that reading textbooks or assessment frameworks alone will result in competent assessment practice. Students and inexperienced practitioners need opportunities to explore and develop the complex set of skill and knowledge requirements presented in textbooks and assessment frameworks, ideally in some form of supervised practice.
- Educators should have a clear rationale for recommending/requiring students/practitioners to read particular textbooks or assessment frameworks.
- Educators need to be aware of the limitations of the textbooks and assessment frameworks they recommend. In particular, an awareness is required of any changes in policy, legislation or expectations of practitioners that might result in some information contained in textbooks or assessment frameworks being outdated or superseded. It may be necessary to make such information known to students/practitioners or recommend supplementary readings that are not subject to such constraints.

Recommendations for authors

- Be explicit as to who the intended audience is. It is reasonable to assume some prior knowledge of practice processes, provided it is made clear that the textbook/assessment framework is not aiming to provide introductory knowledge to basic practice skills. Recommendations for alternate reading could be made for readers seeking out more introductory information on assessment.
- Define concepts such as assessment, for which there is no single definition.
- Include case studies and learning exercises to encourage more active learning.
- Explicitly discuss the theoretical and evidence bases that underpin the writing. Although these might be self-evident to the author, the reader should not have to second guess what they might be.

- Recognise constraints such as word limits, and suggest recommended reading so that the audience has some idea of where to read further on key topics.

1

Introduction

In 2003, the Social Care Institute for Excellence published a report by the authors of this review on the learning and teaching of assessment skills for social work practice.[3] This previous report was primarily focused on how learning and teaching occurred in the classroom and in practice learning settings. In the conclusion, we noted that learning and teaching about assessment can occur through other mediums, and noted the potential of textbooks and assessment frameworks.

Although often criticised for their lack of depth on the topics they cover, in terms of sales and readership, textbooks are often claimed to be highly influential in shaping the understanding of social work students and practitioners. Furthermore, textbooks can have a long life in terms of influence, as it is not uncommon for social workers to refer back to the textbooks they had as students many years before. Indeed, favoured textbooks can often be seen on the desks of practitioners long after they were first published.

Increasingly over the past decade or so, assessment practice in the UK has involved the use of standardised frameworks such as the *Framework for the assessment of children in need and their families.*[4] Moreover, several of these are now widely available due to distribution via the Internet. Consequently, for the many social workers who have no access to professional libraries through their workplaces,[5] such documents may be the most readily obtainable new literature.

This review includes two studies, one concerned with textbooks and the other with assessment frameworks, in an effort to determine just what the reader, especially those who are beginning social work students or unqualified workers, might learn about assessment from such documents. In particular, we focus on how assessment is conceptualised, assessment processes, relevance to the practice context in the UK, the evidence bases that underpin these documents, and the transferability of knowledge.

By bringing together information on a range of textbooks and assessment frameworks, one of the aims of this review is to be a resource for social work educators who are responsible for teaching about assessment in the new social work degrees, especially those who are responsible for developing the curriculum and selecting textbooks. The approach we have taken also provides a model that social work educators might adopt for comparing and selecting learning materials for social work education more generally. Furthermore, some of the findings will have implications for educators who contribute to the education of social work students and/or practitioners through the writing of textbooks and assessment frameworks.

While we realise that the extent of details provided in some sections of our findings may have a relatively limited audience even among social work educators, much of the content is likely to be of interest to a much wider range of people who have an interest in social work assessment, including students, practitioners and service users. Readers can get a feel for the overall findings by looking just at the key points at the end of each section. In addition, the review is designed so that, within the findings section of each study, readers can concentrate on the sections that are of most interest.

Given the potentially diverse readership, the review concludes with three sets of recommendations, with the aim of developing critical development and use of textbooks and assessment frameworks. The first of these is aimed at all readers of textbooks and assessment frameworks, including students, practitioners, service users and educators. The second set of recommendations is aimed at social work educators who use these documents to facilitate learning. Finally, there are recommendations aimed at authors of textbooks and assessment frameworks.

2

Study 1: textbooks

2.1 Introduction

2.1.1 What is the role of textbooks?

Current textbooks are a source of information about contemporary thinking in their subject area[6] and while "there is more to the socialization of students … than merely the textbook literature",[7] a study of textbooks provides an insight into expert thinking on what should be taught. Indeed, it has been proposed that:

> Textbooks are fundamental resources for educators, students and practitioners. Educators often use textbooks to guide course planning and to determine what topics need to be covered. Textbooks convey to students what substantive areas should be understood for competent practice, and the knowledge, attitudes, values and skills believed to be essential for this practice are exemplified in their context. Social workers in the field often turn to texts to review information that is relevant to issues they confront in practice, particularly when they face situations that challenge them. The extent to which content in textbooks is present, accurate, comprehensive, and useful will influence the quality of what is taught to students and what educators and practitioners understand to be important.[8]

Although "good teachers can maximise the use of even a mediocre textbook",[9] textbooks can come to drive the curriculum rather than be an adjunct to other learning activities:[10]

> Introductory sociology books socialize not only students but also the faculty members who teach from them. Indeed, many graduate students and junior faculty members are acculturated to our common disciplinary assumptions by teaching through the chapters of the introductory texts. In this sense pedagogy merges with academic

professionalization, underlining the disciplinary constitutive nature of the textbooks. The books not only reflect our discipline; they also help to reproduce it in the way in which they expose graduate students and faculty to the consensus underlying the dominant approach to epistemology, methodology and theory.[11]

Yet there is often a lack of consensus among educators as to which textbooks they should be promoting. For example, when the syllabus of 32 US graduate social work programmes that taught identifiable courses on groupwork were reviewed, a total of 38 different textbooks were identified, with the number of textbooks used ranging from none to four, with two being most common. One text was used in 13 schools, two in seven schools, and 14 more in between two and five schools. Twenty of the identified textbooks were used in just one of the sample of 32 schools of social work in this study.[12] As the author of this study noted:

> ... there appears to be a variety in the textbooks used for teaching group work. It is interesting that the most frequently used textbook was written by a psychiatrist, not a social worker. In addition, this textbook focuses on long-term psychotherapy groups rather than short-term task-oriented groups so often used in social work group work. However, the results of this study indicate that a number of group work texts authored by social workers are being utilized in schools of social work.[13]

Key points
- Textbooks are an important resource for students, educators and practitioners.
- The content of a textbook reflects an expert opinion about what should be taught.

2.1.2 Critiques of textbooks

Presumably, when a range of textbooks exists in a subject area, each has its own emphases. Textbooks "are conceived, designed and authored by real people with real interests"[14] and the content of a textbook is a statement of cultural politics.[15] For example, a US study that examined inclusion of key legal cases in introductory law textbooks published between 1986 and 1995 found considerable variation as to which were included. Furthermore, whereas some aspects of law were argued by the researchers to be disproportionately covered, other highly significant cases were not included in the 30 most reported:[16]

> ... extensive textbook coverage of a topic implies importance and conveys formal recognition of a subject, while limited coverage may unintentionally trivialize a subject or downplay the importance in students' minds. An absence of coverage may even allow the topic to remain so invisible that it never enters the reader's mind at all. In addition, textbooks offer an organizing framework of ideas for students.[17]

Textbooks may include lengthy discussions of non-core topics (topics typically regarded by textbook authors as requiring at most only brief coverage) or provide too little information to be of use to a practitioner. Alternatively, they may provide basic procedural information but lack relevant contextual knowledge. As Mertens[18] noted in her analysis of textbooks about evaluation, those she reviewed tended to cover the mechanics of evaluation but not the philosophical assumptions that underpinned them. Textbooks that may be generally good, may be deficient or weak in respect of specific concepts.[19] In their reviews of 50 palliative care textbooks, Ferrell et al[20] found that many authors did not address seemingly key issues, including definitions, interdisciplinary working, client choice, confidentiality, and legal and ethical issues. Thus, while textbooks are often viewed uncritically as sources of "legitimate" knowledge,[21]

> ... critics have found that textbooks in nearly every subject and grade level cover too many topics, the writing is superficial, choppy and lacking in depth and breadth (the phenomenon is called "mentioning"), and content wanders between the important and the trivial.[22]

While a lack of information on some topics may simply be due to oversight, editorial constraints can result in deliberate omissions. For example, when the editors of four North American medical textbooks were presented with reviews regarding the lack of useful information they included in respect of end-of-life care in 12 leading causes of death, the editors of two of these texts sought to rectify this shortcoming in their next edition. One other editor's response to the researchers was that the need to cover other material precluded a more detailed coverage of this topic in future editions.[23]

Publishers distribute textbooks for which they expect there to be a sufficient audience to recoup their costs and make a profit,[24] leaving the potential for the quality and utility of information contained therein to be a secondary consideration. Hence, for example, some relatively recently published textbooks may be out of date or overly reliant on old references.[25] Furthermore, textbooks may be more of a reflection of mainstream thinking in a discipline rather than being at the cutting edge.[26] Topics that may be less than adequately discussed or avoided altogether are often those that are controversial or emerging.[27] Wachholz and Mullaly[28] examined the latest editions of all 14 introductory social work texts published in the US over a 10-year period in their exploration of the incorporation of feminist, radical and anti-racist social work scholarship in these mainstream publications. They found that:

> The knowledge contained in textbooks tends to assist in the reproduction of the existing social order and its attendant inequalities along the lines of class, gender and race. This reproduction is aided by the suppression and/or marginalization of scholarship that seeks to challenge or transform it. Certainly, this was the case with the textbooks analyzed for this study. Individual change and liberal reform rather than structural solutions were identified as the means to deal with oppression and inequalities. The introductory social work textbooks appear to contribute to a false consciousness on the part of the reader (i.e. beginning social work students) to participate in the current social order rather than try to change it.[29]

Notwithstanding the lack of consensus as to what this might involve, arguably the task of a textbook in social work is to foster good practice.[30] While the content is undoubtedly important, how it is presented is also critical. The structure of a textbook provides an explicit statement as to what the authors consider to be crucial knowledge for readers. Topics not mentioned in tables of contents (chapter titles and section headings) or indexes may readily be missed by students.[31]

In social work textbooks, it has been proposed that the inclusion of case examples is crucial.[32] However, case studies may be problematic if they promote or perpetuate stereotypes. Studies of North American textbooks in a range of disciplines have revealed biases in respect of gender, race, social class and disability, which may reinforce existing stereotypes and assumptions.[33]

Arguably, a further requirement of a good textbook is that it encourages critical thought:

> … what matters most in a textbook is whether or not it stimulates critical thought. That cannot be done by telling students the correct answers because, far more often than we would like to admit, there are no correct answers.[34]

This would seem particularly important in an era when increasingly busy students sometimes opt to forego class attendance and read whatever textbooks they find in university and agency libraries, the content of which may differ substantially from what is taught in class. After noting some significant problems with Erikson's stages of human development, Milner and O'Byrne note:

> Certainly, social work students love Erikson, but we harbour suspicions that this is because his outline is seductively simple and, all too often, his is the one book to be found on agency shelves when it comes time to write up accounts of practice in theoretical terms.[35]

As textbooks are often selected by teachers who may have only limited knowledge in a particular area, it may well be that choice is determined more by what they consider will appeal to students than an expert appraisal of the quality of the material presented.[36] To this end, several criteria have been suggested for teachers to use in appraising a specific text for one of their classes. These include:

- Is the text up to date and accurate?
- Is it comprehensive?
- Does it adequately and properly portray minority ethnic communities and women?
- Are the objectives, headings and summaries clear?
- Are the contents and index well organised?

- Is it durable enough to last several years?
- What are the outstanding features of the text?
- What are the shortcomings of the text?
- Do the outstanding features strongly override the shortcomings?[37]

A further issue for consideration when adopting a textbook is cultural relevance. The majority of textbooks are produced with the intention of use within their own country[38], which has led to suggestions that a nationalistic bias has resulted in North American sociology ignoring European social theory.[39] Within social work, the need for textbooks that recognise national concerns has also been recognised and within the UK there have been a number of new textbooks that have been produced to support the introduction of the new social work curricula.[40] Indeed, one of the authors of this review has been asked by one of the major publishing houses to identify further areas for the development of new textbooks.

Notwithstanding the extensive use of texts written by nationals within both the UK and the US, publishers often consider the export potential for university-level textbooks. Textbooks that are most likely to be exported are those that transcend local conditions, for example science or mathematics.[41] Nevertheless, some textbooks known to be used in UK social work courses were written elsewhere.

Despite a lack of consensus as to what constitutes assessment,[42] it is a core skill in social work that has been recognised as one of the key areas to be included in each of the curricula for the new social work awards in England,[43] Northern Ireland,[44] Scotland[45] and Wales,[46] and is known to feature in many introductory social work textbooks. This review seeks to review social work textbooks currently being used in the UK in relation to the assessment process.

Key points
- Textbooks should be carefully evaluated before being recommended to students.
- A range of textbooks may suggest a lack of consensus about key topics to be covered.
- Textbooks may have insufficient information on some topics, be out of date, not culturally relevant or have other deficiencies.

- Textbooks may reflect the status quo or mainstream thinking rather than being at the cutting edge. As such, they may reflect what publishers believe will sell.

2.2 Method

2.2.1 Criteria for inclusion

Previous studies of textbooks have utilised a range of criteria for the selection of their samples. What is evident, however, is that there have been clear rules for inclusion.[47] One study of how social work textbooks dealt with the concept of validity involved a sample of textbooks published after a certain date that were held in the private libraries of the researcher and his colleagues,[48] whereas others have restricted their reviews to books currently in print.[49] Some studies of textbooks have involved examinations of online publishing industry data on sales of textbooks and the selection of the most current editions and most sold titles. Copies of these were then requested from the relevant publishers.[50] Others have selected a small number of books that were known to be widely used,[51] which have been marketed as being introductory to the discipline[52] or which the authors had indicated were developed for use in generalist social work practice courses.[53] Criteria for inclusion have also included the country in which a textbook has been published.[54]

The selection criteria for this study were determined as follows:

- social work textbooks that included a substantial section (one or more chapters, or identifiable sections if there were no chapters) on assessment or were entirely focused on assessment
- textbooks with a generalist focus, that is, not focusing on a specific population (for example children) or problem (for example substance misuse)
- currently available for sale within the UK
- published between 1994 and 2003
- where multiple editions existed, the most recently published edition.

2.2.2 Identification of sample texts

Once the criteria had been determined, a list of introductory social work textbooks was identified by the authors. These books were then inspected to determine whether or not they included a chapter (or distinct section if there were no chapters) with a specific focus on assessment. Subsequent efforts to augment this sample involved searching relevant shelves at the University of Glasgow library, and at three Glasgow bookshops known to sell social work textbooks.[55]

Ten textbooks that included one or more chapters on assessment were identified. These were:

- *Anti-oppressive practice: Social care and the law* (1995), by Jane Dalrymple and Beverley Burke[56]
- *The Blackwell encyclopaedia of social work* (2000), edited by Martin Davies.[57] This included entries on assessment by (a) Sonia Jackson,[58] (b) Leonne Griggs[59] and (c) Hazel Kemshall and Charlotte Knight[60]
- *Constructive social work: Towards a new practice* (2000), by Nigel Parton and Patrick O'Byrne[61]
- *Critical practice in social work* (2001), edited by Robert Adams, Lena Dominelli and Malcolm Payne.[62] This included chapters on assessment by (a) Judith Milner and Patrick O'Byrne,[63] and (b) Terence O'Sullivan[64]
- *Direct social work practice: Theory and skills* (2002, 6th edn), by Dean H. Hepworth, Ronald H. Rooney and Jo Ann Larsen[65]
- *Social work: Critical theory and practice* (2002), by Jan Fook[66]
- *Social work practice: An introduction* (1998, 3rd edn), by Veronica Coulshed and Joan Orme[67]
- *Social work practice: Assessment, planning, intervention and review* (2003), by Jonathan Parker and Greta Bradley[68]
- *Social work processes* (1999, 6th edn), by Beulah R. Compton and Burt Galaway[69]
- *Social work skills: A practice handbook* (2000), by Pamela Trevithick.[70]

Textbooks reviewed that did not include a chapter on assessment are listed in Appendix 3.

Six books that focus specifically on assessment were also identified. These were:

- *The art of assessment* (1997), by Laura Middleton[71]
- *Assessment in social work* (2002, 2nd edn), by Judith Milner and Patrick O'Byrne[72]
- *Good practice in risk assessment and risk management 1* (1996), edited by Hazel Kemshall and Jacki Pritchard[73]
- *Good practice in risk assessment and risk management 2: Protection, rights and responsibilities* (1997), edited by Hazel Kemshall and Jacki Pritchard[74]
- *Social assessment theory and practice: A multi-disciplinary framework* (1998), by Derek Clifford[75]
- *Social work and social problems: Working towards social inclusion and social change* (2000), by Gerald Smale, Graham Tuson and Daphne Statham.[76]

One further book, the title of which had suggested that it may be within scope, was *Risk assessment in social care and social work*, edited by Phyllida Parsloe.[77] Closer inspection, however, revealed this book to be an edited series of essays reviewing research about the nature and predictors of risk, rather than a primary focus on assessment per se.

2.2.3 Analysis framework

A standardised proforma was developed for analysis of the content of each of the selected textbooks.[78] Data entered onto the proforma for each textbook included factual information (for example, number of pages devoted to the topic of assessment), content relating to issues of prominence in social work and social work education in the UK (for example, policy and legislation, anti-discriminatory/anti-oppressive practice, evidence-based practice), pedagogical issues (for example, inclusion of case studies or suggested further reading), and a subjective impression of the potential of each textbook in relation to the learning and teaching of assessment.

The initial proforma was trialled and then modified as additional categories emerged that had not been anticipated but were potentially relevant. Expert advice was also sought in relation to the categories for the proforma.[79] It also became clear that slight modifications were needed for analyses of chapters in edited collections and authored books, and for analyses of chapters versus whole books. In respect of chapters in authored books, the proforma collected data on the following categories:

- title
- author(s)
- author'(s) affiliation(s) at time of publication
- edition
- cost
- intended audience
- number of pages – total
- number of pages – assessment
- key headings within chapters on assessment
- definitions of assessment
- timing of assessment
- theoretical underpinnings
- information obtained during the assessment process
- risk assessment
- multidisciplinary assessment
- involvement of users and carers in the process
- user and carer perspectives of the assessment process
- evidence bases
- inclusion of case studies
- languages other than English and use of interpreters
- anti-discriminatory/anti-oppressive practice
- legislation/legal frameworks
- accuracy
- comprehensiveness
- durability
- transferability
- recommended further reading
- learning exercises
- outstanding features
- shortcomings.

The completed proformas for chapters on assessment can be found in Appendix 1, and the proformas for books focusing on assessment in Appendix 2.

2.3 Findings

The process of identifying chapters on assessment revealed three predominant structures of generalist social work textbooks. These were textbooks in which material was organised around (a) social work processes, (b) theories, and (c) practice settings/client groups. While content on assessment may be found in all three types of textbook, only in the first of these were distinct chapters on assessment to be found. In textbooks that introduce the reader to a number of theories or practice settings, assessment may be briefly mentioned in a number of chapters, that is, diffused across the textbook. Such diffusion may underlie the observation that:

> Having agreed on the centrality of assessment in the social work process, texts then dismiss the subject in a few pages. Apart from some brief homilies on counterchecking facts and hypotheses and the necessity of reassessing wherever appropriate, most writers make a list of information-yielding sources and then depart from the subject to other aspects of the social work process.[80]

Such assertions are only partly borne out by this study. While the briefest writing on assessment was the total of six pages or just 1.6% of the total number of text pages in *The Blackwell encyclopaedia of social work*,[81] other entries were both longer and comprised a greater proportion of pages. The number of pages, and the proportion of the total number of text pages (that is, excluding indexes and appendices) devoted to assessment for the 10 books for which assessment was the focus of a limited number of chapters is shown in Table 1, and ranged up to 140 pages. Six of these books devoted approximately 10% or more of the total number of pages of text to the topic of assessment.

The total number of pages on assessment in some of these textbooks would be in the same ballpark as some of the textbooks that solely focus on assessment. The 48 large pages (approximately B5 paper size) about assessment in Compton and Galaway[82] and the 61 large pages in Parker

Table 1: Social work textbooks that include one or more chapters on assessment: number of pages on assessment and proportion of total textbook

Author(s)/editor(s)	Number of pages – assessment	Number of pages – text total	Proportion of pages on assessment (%)
Adams, Dominelli and Payne	17	311	5.5
Compton and Galaway	48	508	9.5
Coulshed and Orme	29	234	12.4
Dalrymple and Burke	12	165	7.3
Davies	6	380	1.6
Fook	11	168	6.5
Hepworth, Rooney and Larsen	140	600	23.3
Parker and Bradley	61	136	44.9
Parton and O'Byrne	18	187	9.6
Trevithick	19	176	10.8

and Bradley[83] arguably included more text on the topic than the 70 small pages (approximately A5 paper size) of Middleton's[84] short text, which focused exclusively on assessment. Furthermore, the 140 large pages by Hepworth et al[85] says probably more on assessment than the 191 smaller pages of the book by Milner and O'Byrne.[86]

Key points
- The social work textbooks examined vary considerably in the amount of content they include on assessment, ranging from six to 140 pages.
- Most textbooks had around 10% of content about assessment, but this ranged from less than 2% to 45%.

2.3.1 Audience

The textbooks that met the inclusion criteria for this study were not all aimed at the same audience. While some were clearly pitched at a level appropriate to beginning social work students and made few assumptions about prior knowledge of the reader, others were pitched at a much more advanced level – at students close to qualifying as social workers or qualified workers.[87]

While the majority of textbooks reviewed sold for under £20, the most expensive[88] cost more than £50, which is likely to restrict its purchase to practitioners and libraries.

Three of the textbooks were written outside the UK; two, Compton and Galaway[89] and Hepworth et al[90] in the North American context, the former of these including authors based in both the US and Canada at the time of publication. These were the two largest textbooks overall, with the largest number of pages devoted to assessment in books not solely focused on this topic. However, readers wanting to locate assessment within the UK policy and practice contexts would need to obtain this information elsewhere. The emphasis of these two books is somewhat different, as they engage with current debates and emphases within North American social work. For example, risk assessment and statutory intervention receive little attention in these books, with the client being referred to as "the applicant", with an implicit assumption that clients seek services that do not necessarily reflect the strong emphasis of statutory social work in the UK, where social work clients are often involuntary. Some particularly North American concerns that are discussed include the debate as to whether or not social workers should use the American Psychiatric Association's *DSM-IV* classification of mental disorders[91] in assessments, and concerns over the term 'diagnosis'.

The remaining textbook written outside the UK was by Fook,[92] who is Australian. Although she does not explicitly mention UK policies and legislation, some of her emphases, such as working in partnership with service users and carers, are consistent with current policy and practice in the UK. She also draws considerably on recent social work literature from the UK.

Key points

- Textbooks may be aimed at different audiences from beginning social work students to advanced students or practitioners, with varying assumptions as to the extent of prior knowledge of readers.
- Textbooks published in other countries may not reflect UK policy and practice emphases.

2.3.2 What is assessment?

Although most textbooks provide some definition of assessment, a common understanding may not be readily apparent to a novice reader. However, most of the definitions provided relate to one or more of the five stages of the framework for assessment proposed by Milner and O'Byrne:

1. Preparation. Deciding who to see, what data will be relevant, what the purpose is and the limits of the task are.
2. Data collection. People are met and engaged with, difference gaps are addressed, and empowerment and choice are safeguarded as we come to the task with respectful uncertainty and a research mentality.
3. Weighing the data. Current social and psychological theory and research findings that are part of every social worker's learning are drawn on to answer the questions 'Is there a problem?' and 'How serious is it?'....
4. Analysing the data. One or more of the analytic maps are then used to interpret the data and to seek to gain an understanding of them in order to develop their ideas for intervention....
5. Utilising the analysis. This is the stage in which judgments are finalised....[93]

For example, in relation to defining the task, it has been proposed that:

> Assessment is an ongoing process, in which the client participates, the purpose of which is to understand people in relation to their environment; it is a basis for planning what needs to be done to maintain, improve or bring about change in the person, the environment or both.[94]

This might involve assessing risk,[95] or ascertaining needs.[96] While some textbooks defined assessment in relation to individual clients only,[97] others acknowledged a wider scope, including groups and even the potential for community-wide assessments.[98] Hence, it has been suggested that:

> Workers have to develop an understanding of the nature of the particular social problem being tackled, and the feasibility of different kinds of solution and their possible consequences. Realistic assessment has
>
> - to address the whole of the task
> - to engage in ongoing negotiations with the full range of people involved in specific problems and their possible solutions
> - to address both the change, care and social control tasks
> - to go beyond the individualisation of social problems as the focus for assessment and intervention.[99]

Rather than defining the parameters, other writers are more concerned with processes of collecting and analysing data, such that:

> Assessment – the collection and processing of data to provide information for use in making decisions about the nature of the problem and what is to be done about it – is a cognitive, thinking process; it involves thinking about data that have been collected. The outcome of assessment is a service plan, which provides a definition of the problem for work, objectives or solutions to be achieved, and an action plan to accomplish the objectives.[100]

Still others have defined assessment in terms of analysing data and developing hypotheses:

> … a fluid and dynamic process that involves receiving, analysing and synthesizing new information as it emerges during the entire course of a given case.[101]

Similarly, it has been suggested that:

> … assessment, intervention and service delivery are essentially the same exercise.[102]

Finally, the definitions of assessment in some textbooks emphasised the process of decision making, typically involving professional judgements. For example:

> Assessment can be described as a process of professional judgement or appraisal of the situation, circumstances and behaviour of the offender.[103]

Interestingly, however, a few writers point out the subjective nature of professional assessments. For example:

> Assessment is a basis for decision making and different types of assessment can be distinguished by their purpose…. The result of any assessment is a particular representation of reality….[104]

And as has been noted, that reality is typically that of the professional:

> We also need to acknowledge that the assessment made may primarily represent the perspective of the professional worker making it. Assessment making, in this sense, is no more or less than the professional worker constructing his or her own narrative of the problem situation.[105]

In only one textbook did the initial definitions of assessment make any mention of the fact that formal assessments are usually written.[106] Possibly this reflects the fact that many textbooks suggested assessment to be an ongoing process rather than a determination at a particular point in time.

Key points
- Most, but not all, of the textbooks provided a definition of assessment.
- There is no common definition of assessment.

2.3.3 The assessment process

It is expected that qualified social workers have sufficient knowledge to conduct assessments of service users and carers. However, while some of the book chapters reviewed provided readers with some philosophical underpinnings of assessment[107] or an introduction to some current practice debates within the UK,[108] the student wanting information on specific assessment tools or about the process of actually conducting an assessment may need to look elsewhere.

Several different theoretical underpinnings to assessment were proposed. These included:

- behavioural approaches[109]
- an exchange model[110]
- narrative approaches[111]
- postmodern and critical thinking[112]
- psychodynamic approaches[113]
- solution-focused approaches[114]
- strengths perspective[115]
- systems theory[116]
- task-centred approaches.[117]

The range of theoretical underpinnings would seem likely to account for the diverse advice given to readers on what information they should be collecting in assessments.

Some books propose specific lists of questions,[118] domains[119] or assessment tools[120] that assessors might use to obtain information from service users and carers. A few textbooks make reference to the specific demands of legislation or widely used assessment frameworks.[121]

Others are less prescriptive, calling for a critical rather than a mechanistic use of checklists.[122] For example, Coulshed and Orme[123] noted that, although the social work literature includes extensive lists of different types of information that have been proposed as necessary to obtain during assessments, what denotes a skilled assessor is the ability to collect sufficient relevant information for the specific context. Likewise, Middleton[124] stresses the need to collect pertinent information, noting that not to impose such a restriction is intrusive, and can result in invasions of privacy and time wasting. Fook[125] and Clifford,[126] who both portray the assessment task as research, remind their readers that other forms of information, beyond those gained through discussions with service users, might also contribute relevant insights.

Changes in emphasis over time in respect of assessments are noted by a few writers. For example, it is noted that the assessment of offenders has moved from "the traditional psychoanalytic and diagnostic approach ... to those criminogenic factors which research has indicated are associated with offending".[127] Elsewhere, the change in philosophy from resource-led to needs-led assessments, as a result of the introduction of the NHS and Community Care Act 1990, was mentioned.[128] One change of emphasis that a number of writers endorse is a greater focus on strengths rather than what has often been the prevailing practice of focusing on problems.[129]

One apparent change in assessment practice within the UK in recent years is a more overt emphasis on risk assessment. Indeed, risk assessment was the focus for two textbooks reviewed for this study.[130] The remaining textbooks, which focused on assessment more generally, approached the subject of risk in a wide range of ways, with no obvious trends in respect of when and where books were published. A number of other textbooks devote entire chapters[131] or substantial sections of a chapter[132] to risk assessment, and/or included mentions of risk assessment in several chapters. Another approach is to discuss risk assessment only in respect of particular scenarios, such as offending[133] or suicide.[134] Alternatively, some textbooks will mention that social workers may be involved in assessing risk but provide little or no practical information as to what this might entail.[135]

Some of the books and chapters that were reviewed made little or no mention of risk or risk assessment. Yet, in a couple of instances there is content that could be understood as pertaining to risk assessment and management, such as discussions about 'social control'[136] and a section entitled 'Forming decisions and making judgements'.[137] Nevertheless, in a couple of the textbooks in which we had reviewed the chapters ostensibly on assessment, there were more extensive discussions of work assessment in other chapters.[138]

A further aspect of the assessment process that we thought might be discussed in social work textbooks is multidisciplinary assessment. While it is an expectation in the UK that some types of assessments, for example of children in need, and the shared assessment process for older persons, will involve professionals from a range of disciplines in addition to social work, only a few textbooks noted these legislative or policy requirements.[139] However, while recognising that a range of stakeholders may be involved in an assessment is an important first step,[140] consideration of the implications for both clients and workers would seem crucial.[141]

In the context of writing about assessment, some textbooks included substantial sections on multidisciplinary working.[142] However, while the overall configuration of topics within textbooks resulted in some textbooks considering multidisciplinary working in separate chapters from those on assessment,[143] there was an apparent absence of material about multidisciplinary working in other books.[144]

Key points

- Several different theories of assessment were proposed in the textbooks.
- Details of what information should be collected and how it should be collected varied considerably. While some textbooks provided few practical details about how to conduct an assessment, others were far more prescriptive.
- A few textbooks discussed changes in assessment practice in recent years.
- There was no common approach to the topics of risk and risk assessment. While some textbooks discussed these in considerable detail, others provided no more than a brief mention or discussed these ideas in chapters other than those focusing on assessment.
- Despite legislative requirements for multidisciplinary working, there was little or no content on multidisciplinary assessments in several textbooks.

2.3.4 Involvement of service users and carers in the assessment process

The potential involvement of service users and carers varied considerably in the textbooks reviewed. Some writers stressed that working in partnership with users and carers is critical.[145] This includes not only involving children and carers as sources of information,[146] but also ensuring that the voices of service users and carers are given prominence in assessment reports that are subsequently produced.[147]

Other writers were more circumspect, even indicating the lack of agreement within the profession of social work regarding the extent that service users should be involved in decision making.[148] For example, some textbooks,[149] while noting the importance of ascertaining the views of service users and carers, also acknowledge that legislative requirements may result in assessments that are more a reflection of the worker's professional judgement than the expressed preferences of service users and carers. One of the tensions around the limits of service-user involvement is that:

> Despite the principle that individuals should be allowed to assess the risks to themselves … should an elderly person be found to have died alone at home it is likely that social work will be found culpable.[150]

While considering the involvement of service users and carers as crucial, Fook[151] makes a helpful distinction between obtaining maximum exchange of information and maximum agreement between professionals and clients. A six-point framework for assessment proposed by Dalrymple and Burke provides some guidance towards meeting the former of these objectives:

1. Assessment should involve those being assessed.
2. Openness and honesty should permeate the process.
3. Assessment should involve the sharing of values and concerns.
4. There should be acknowledgement of the structural context of the process.
5. The process should be about questioning the basis of the reasons for proposed action, and all those involved should consider alternative courses of action.
6. Assessment should incorporate the different perspectives of the people involved.[152]

It was also noted that the involvement of children and their carers in the assessment process is a particularly British emphasis:

> It is a legal requirement in Britain, as well as good practice, that children should be encouraged and enabled to express their ideas

about their own situation and where they should live, an aspect of child care that was seriously neglected in the past and is still absent from discussion in much of the US literature.[153]

This was certainly true of the two North American texts that were reviewed. Although client self-determination is mentioned, assessment is very much portrayed as an activity conducted by professional social workers.[154] Moreover, working in partnership with service users and carers is suggested as an option rather than an imperative.[155]

Key points
- The potential involvement of service users and carers varied considerably.
- Some writers stressed that working in partnership with users and carers is critical, whereas others, while noting the importance of ascertaining the views of service users and carers, acknowledged legislative requirements that may result in assessments that are more a reflection of the worker's professional judgement.
- The active involvement of children and their carers in the assessment process is a particularly British emphasis.

2.3.5 Legislation and policy contexts

The chapters and books on assessment reviewed for this study took four distinct approaches in respect to the legal and policy contexts in which assessment occurs. These varying approaches reveal a tension between being a textbook which is explicitly up to date by incorporating many references to contemporary policies and legislation, and being a textbook which is more about concepts, and hence more durable.

The first approach involves explicit discussion of relevant legislation,[156] and as such, are the least durable due to being most at risk of becoming rapidly outdated. In respect of some of the older textbooks, there been considerable changes in legislation, and even a change of government in Westminster since being written.[157] Although all of these books were written within the UK, none made any reference to the fact that some legislation does not apply across the UK. In particular, it would seem that a close fit with English legislation and requirements limits transferability of these textbooks to UK countries other than England.

The authors of one book, which marketed itself as a resource for students on the new social work degree,[158] did not acknowledge that they were only addressing the requirements for social work education in England,[159] and that there are some variations in Scotland,[160] Northern Ireland[161] and Wales.[162] The confining of references to specific legislation to within a few pages may enhance transferability to other countries.[163]

The second approach stresses the need to be aware of legislative requirements that impact on the assessment process, but makes only brief mention of specific legislation and policies.[164] Readers would need to look elsewhere for details about these pieces of legislation. By focusing on general concepts rather than specific legislation, policies or service providers, these textbooks are more durable, and have greater transferability to other countries, than those that discuss particular legislation. There is also the potential to discuss concepts that have yet to be covered by legislation, such as a very pertinent discussion around access to client records that were written prior to the promulgation of the Data Protection Act 1998.[165] Nevertheless, readers may be reminded that the process of assessment may change to reflect changes in legislation and policy.[166] Such reminders are pertinent, given that draft documents are finalised and gain status, and that organisations responsible for overseeing policy guidelines may change over time.[167]

The third approach also notes the important of an awareness of the legislative context, but does not discuss or even name specific legislation.[168] The fourth approach, which was only observed in textbooks written in North America and Australia, was not to mention legislation or policy contexts.[169] This may reflect the authors' contexts of working in countries with federal systems of government where much of the legislation that affects social work is made by state legislatures, and hence is not consistent across the country.

Key points
- Explicit discussion of relevant legislation may result in textbooks that are at risk of becoming rapidly outdated.
- Textbooks that focus on general concepts rather than specific legislation, policies or service providers date less quickly, and have greater transferability to other countries, than those that discuss particular legislation.

2.3.6 Anti-discriminatory and anti-oppressive practice

As with other areas of content in relation to assessment, the information presented in the reviewed textbooks about anti-discriminatory and anti-oppressive practice varied considerably. One of the six books that focused specifically on assessment in our sample included an entire chapter on anti-oppressive practice.[170] A number of other authors also promote anti-oppressive practice as an imperative.[171]

Interestingly, only authors from the UK use the terms 'anti-discriminatory' or 'anti-oppressive' practice, although textbooks written elsewhere discussed issues of difference, including race/ethnicity and gender.[172] Yet not all UK authors explicitly use these terms either, with some writers writing chapters that are consistent with the concepts, but minus the language, of anti-discriminatory/anti-oppressive practice.[173] As Clifford, who prefers to write about "social division" notes, "I use the term 'anti-oppressive' sparingly because of its adoption as a term of abuse in some quarters".[174] Parker and Bradley[175] take the concept further through the inclusion of details about using a "culturagram", which they suggest can assist gaining understanding of the meaning and impact of culture on individuals and families. This is a paper and pencil graphical approach to collecting information in a manner not dissimilar to using genograms[176] and ecomaps[177] in the assessment process.

Despite the fact that most of the textbooks sought to bring issues of disadvantage and discrimination to the attention of the reader, only two of the textbooks reviewed discussed assessing clients whose first language is not English.[178] In general, the implicit assumption seems to be that social work clients speak sufficient English to discuss their problems. For example, Parker and Bradley suggest:

> It is also important to be mindful of language and communication issues, especially where English is a second language. Social workers will need to ask careful, concrete questions and be prepared to repeat or put certain questions to one side. Summaries of discussion, paraphrasing and sharing written copies of the information can help in developing good practice.[179]

However, the possibility of using an interpreter is not mentioned. Indeed, only one textbook[180] mentioned using interpreters in the assessment process, including signing interpreters for deaf clients. This text also made a number of helpful points for working with people whose first language is not English when an interpreter is not used. These include the possibility of clients being less expressive and being less able to articulate their problems in English. It is suggested that social workers need to speak slowly, in simple terms and allow more time for clients to think and respond to questions.

As it was possible that English as a second language and interpreters were more likely to be considered elsewhere in textbooks than in relation to assessment, the indexes of the remaining textbooks were examined, but these identified only one textbook that included mentions of these issues.[181] However, such omissions may well reflect assessment practice in the UK. Parker and Bradley reproduce an example front-sheet for an assessment, which includes a range of demographic information including ethnicity and religion, but makes no mention of languages spoken or proficiency in English.[182]

Key points
- Very few textbooks included a chapter on anti-oppressive practice in assessment.
- Several textbooks included writing that is consistent with the concepts, but minus the terms 'anti-discriminatory practice' or 'anti-oppressive practice'.
- Very few textbooks acknowledged issues associated with assessing clients whose first language is not English.

2.3.7 Evidence bases

In an era when evidence-based practice is being increasingly promoted in the UK, the extent to which the various textbooks engaged with research evidence varied considerably. Milner and O'Byrne[183] explicitly discuss the adequacy of the research evidence to support the various approaches they propose. Others who also explicitly discuss research evidence, including its adequacy, include Clifford,[184] Compton and Galaway,[185] Hepworth et al[186] and Parker and Bradley.[187] O'Sullivan[188] includes a useful section on how research findings can be used in risk assessment, and it is noted that the 'Looking After Children' materials[189] and current approaches to assessing offenders[190] were developed in response to issues identified in research.

While the notion of needing to base assessments on research and not just on unsubstantiated assumptions is actively encouraged in a few textbooks,[191] others include little or no explicit discussion of research evidence.[192] This does not necessarily mean that research evidence has not been referred to, but rather it is not made explicit to the reader which if any of the references on which a chapter or book is based are research evidence or theoretical writings.[193] None of the textbooks explicitly classified references according to type (research evidence, theoretical writing, and so on), let alone typologised research evidence. Consequently, in some textbooks, we were only able to recognise that the authors were basing their writings on research findings if by chance the original research was familiar to us.

For some authors, however, legislation or legal precedents were proposed as the basis for social work action rather than research evidence per se.[194] While it is possible that research evidence also informed these writings, any such thinking is not made explicit and hence it is difficult to positively identify how research findings are influencing proposed practice.

Key points
- Only a few textbooks explicitly discussed research findings.
- No textbook classified references according to whether or not they were evidence based on research.

2.3.8 Pedagogy

As a passive method of learning, reading is likely to be more effective if combined with some form of active learning.[195] While students attending classes in educational institutions typically have recommended reading supplemented by lectures, discussions and other learning activities, some students look to their textbooks as the primary source for their learning. Hence, one way in which textbooks may enhance the learning of their readers is to include some form of learning exercises that encourage more active engagement with the material than just reading. Seven of the reviewed textbooks included some form of learning activities in relation to their chapters on assessment. These were provided either at points throughout the text[196] or at the end of each chapter.[197] While these were usually aimed at students or practitioners directly, one text included exercises that educators and training staff could conduct with groups.[198]

In applied disciplines such as social work, it is not uncommon to demonstrate the use of theory in practice through the use of case studies. Almost all of the textbooks reviewed used case studies to illustrate the material presented on assessment. As to how case studies were integrated into the text, this varied considerably. Some chapters[199] were structured around case studies to enable explicit demonstrations of the integration of theory and practice. Clifford[200] used a similar approach, structuring several chapters of his book around the assessment of different members of the one family. Other approaches involved inclusion of multiple brief case studies,[201] and the inclusion of extended case studies midway through or at the end of the chapters.[202] Kemshall and Pritchard[203] conclude their first volume on risk assessment with a chapter comprising 11 case examples, while Hepworth et al[204] include examples of detailed assessment reports. While it is likely that some of the case studies included in these textbooks were fictional and developed specifically to illustrate particular points, Dalrymple and Burke[205] include material from a number of cases that were in the public arena as a result of court appearances.

A third device that a textbook may incorporate to stimulate learning is to recommend further reading material to the interested reader. This was provided in 10 of the 16 books reviewed. While this would often be as a list at the end of a chapter, a few authors made suggestions for further reading at the points at which issues emerged in the text. Hepworth et al[206] also include assessment tools and other resources that are available via the Internet.

The inclusion of additional reading is not necessarily of great help to a student wanting to learn more about assessment. Parton and O'Byrne[207] include a six-page list of further reading at the end of their textbook, but this is delineated into sections concerned with specific populations and problems, and does not specifically identify further reading about assessment. Another textbook[208] provides only the page numbers of a section of a book published in 1974 for readers wanting to know more about one specific issue.

In summary, all of the textbooks used at least one of the pedagogical devices (learning exercises, case studies, recommended reading), but only two used all of these. The use of these pedagogical devices is summarised in Table 2.

Key points
- Almost all social work textbooks included case examples. However, these were used in a range of ways.
- Exercises to stimulate learning and recommendations for further reading would appear to be somewhat optional in social work textbooks.

2.3.9 Service user and carer perspectives

None of the contributions on assessment in the reviewed textbooks was prepared by persons who identified themselves as writing from the perspective of a service user or carer. This reflects social work textbooks more generally, where with few exceptions,[209] the dominant perspective is that of the professional social worker, with service users and carers being the 'other' who is assessed. Only one textbook acknowledged the possibility that readers might have experienced being assessed.[210] Thus, when the reader is presented with the perspectives of service users and carers, this may be as they are perceived by professionals.[211] Only a couple of textbooks included quotes from service users, telling of their experiences of being assessed.[212] One of these books also included details about a court case in which a service user appealed against the result of an assessment.[213]

A few textbooks completely disregarded the issue of service user and carer perspectives.[214] Furthermore, several of those that made some mention of this sought to encourage readers to make an effort to understand what it is that service users and carers are experiencing, rather than providing them with examples from actual clients.[215] However, such exhortations are usually framed in respect of what it is generally like to be in receipt of social work services rather than the specific experience of being assessed. Perhaps the most useful contributions in respect of seeking to understand the experiences of service users and carers are the two textbooks that included explicit discussion on seeking user feedback[216] and evaluating service user satisfaction.[217]

Table 2: Use of pedagogical aids in social work textbooks that include one or more chapters on assessment

Author(s)/editor(s)	Learning exercises	Case studies	Recommended reading
Textbooks including chapters on assessment			
Adams, Dominelli and Payne		✓	✓
Compton and Galaway	✓	✓	
Coulshed and Orme		✓	✓
Dalrymple and Burke	✓	✓	
Davies			✓
Fook	✓	✓	
Hepworth, Rooney and Larsen		✓	✓
Parker and Bradley	✓	✓	✓
Parton and O'Byrne			✓
Trevithick		✓	✓
Textbooks focusing on assessment			
Clifford	✓	✓	
Kemshall and Pritchard (1996)	✓	✓	
Kemshall and Pritchard (1997)	✓	✓	✓
Middleton		✓	✓
Milner and O'Byrne		✓	✓
Smale, Tuson and Statham		✓	

Key points

- None of the textbooks reviewed were written by authors identifying themselves as service users or carers.
- Only a couple of textbooks included first-hand feedback from service users and carers on the experience of being assessed.
- Several textbooks nevertheless encouraged readers to seek to understand the experience of being assessed from the perspective of service users and carers.

2.4 Discussion

This study sought to examine the extent to which textbooks can be used to facilitate learning about assessment by social work and social care students and professionals. We found considerable variety in the textbooks that we reviewed in respect of the extent of detail and topics covered. While some of these differences reflect changes over time or of authors working in countries with differing emphases on social work practice and education, others may well reflect the lack of a common conceptualisation of the assessment task. In respect of chapters on assessment that are found in larger introductory textbooks, space requirements may result in only key features of the assessment process being highlighted by authors. It should be noted, however, that the majority of textbooks referred the interested reader to additional books or articles on assessment.

As this study included books in print published over a 10-year timeframe, it has been possible to observe changes in emphasis in assessment practice in the UK over that decade. Such changes include a move from resource-led to needs-led assessment, more explicit discussion about research evidence, the introduction of the *Framework for the assessment of children in need and their families*[218] and changes in legislation. Changes in the curriculum for qualifying social work education from the Central Council for Education and Training in Social Work's (CCETSW) Diploma of Social Work[219] to the new requirements for a social work degree in England[220] were also apparent. Nevertheless, there would appear to be a tension between being explicitly up to date with many references to contemporary policies and legislation, and being a textbook that is more about concepts and hence more durable. Despite these changes, some issues, such as principles of anti-discriminatory/anti-oppressive practice and working in partnership with service users and carers, were just as likely to be addressed by books published around a decade ago as those published in the past couple of years.

To some extent, the findings may reflect the methodology adopted for this study, in particular, the approach of selecting textbooks that included readily identifiable chapters on assessment and reviewing those chapters in isolation. Although this is not dissimilar to the way in which many students read for essays and assignments, that is, reading only those sections of books that immediately seem most pertinent, this can result in an analysis of chapters that is not an accurate reflection of the complete volume of which they are a part. For example, although Coulshed and Orme[221] do not discuss the use of interpreters when assessing clients from non-English speaking backgrounds who have limited English skills, this topic is discussed elsewhere in their textbook.

It is possible that there were additional textbooks that met the inclusion criteria, but were not readily identifiable using our search strategies. For example, from our experiences as external examiners for various social work programmes, we would suggest that there are some regional differences in use of textbooks within the UK. In particular, it is our impression that the North American textbooks[222] may be used more widely in Scotland than in England. Conversely, as our search included examining textbooks in libraries and bookshops in Glasgow, we may have omitted textbooks that are little known in Scotland but are used elsewhere in the UK.

For practical purposes, a 10-year timeframe with a cut-off date of 2003 was set for this study. This corresponds with a 10-year period that was used to determine scope in a recent North American study of introductory social work textbooks.[223] Nevertheless, it is recognised that new textbooks in social work are published on an almost continuous basis, and there is at least one new textbook published in the UK since this time that focuses specifically on assessment.[224] With hindsight, we would also recognise that this timeframe resulted in the exclusion of two relevant British textbooks published in 1993 and still widely in use. One of these was *Empowerment, assessment, care management and the skilled worker* by Smale et al,[225] which is a primary text in respect of the exchange model of assessment. We note, however, that the exchange model is also the key theoretical underpinning for their later textbook,[226] which is part of this study. The other excluded textbook was Taylor and Devine's *Assessing needs and planning care in social work.*[227]

A further limitation of this study is that it only considered textbooks that have a recognisable chapter or distinct section on assessment. Such books tend to be framed around the social work task. There are, however, other ways in which introductory social work textbooks are organised, and in these, processes such as assessment may be embedded throughout, recurring in a number of chapters. For example, introductory textbooks on social work theory such as Payne's *Modern social work theory*[228] and Stepney and Ford's *Social work models, methods and theories*[229] both include brief mentions of assessment in a number of chapters, each of which is concerned with different theories for practice. Similarly, Davies' *The Blackwell companion to social work*[230] is just one of many books that could provide valuable contextual knowledge, which may arguably be just as essential as knowledge about the assessment process.

Although we did not tightly define what made a textbook a social work textbook, our working definition was that the target population was specifically social work students and/or practitioners and that the purpose of the book was primarily education rather than reporting on research. Hence, textbooks that were aimed more broadly at a range of health and social care professionals[231] were considered out of scope for this particular study, although we would recognise that their content on assessment may be very relevant for social work students and practitioners.

Conversely, selection of books in this sample does not imply any judgement as to their suitability for teaching UK students about social work assessment. In particular, it has been suggested to us that we should have confined the scope of this study to textbooks published within the UK and excluded textbooks written elsewhere, even though they are being used in some UK social work programmes. While we may question the relevance of some of the content in such textbooks, their exclusion would have removed the opportunity to (a) critique these textbooks and compare them with their British counterparts, and (b) identify British emphases in the assessment process. In an era when considerable numbers of overseas social workers are being recruited to work in the UK,[232] it would seem important to recognise that the practice of social work is affected by cultural and policy contexts rather than being universal. Yet, perhaps an even more pressing reason for not excluding overseas textbooks is the fact that (as the next study in Chapter Three demonstrates) the *Framework for the assessment of children in need and their families*[233] sources its definition of assessment from an edition of Compton and Galaway's *Social work processes*.[234] It is possible that the diligent student who is following up references in this widely used framework may therefore actively seek out a copy of this textbook.

However, it is not just overseas textbooks that may be problematic in some respects. In many textbooks, it was unclear as to the extent to which the advice contained therein was based on research evidence. Furthermore, although there is now widespread recognition across the UK that the voices of service users and carers need to be heard within social work education,[235] most textbooks had little or no content about the experience of being assessed from the perspective of service users and carers, despite a growing literature that throws light on this subject.[236] Our sample of textbooks also made little mention of the fact that assessments are increasingly being conducted on a multidisciplinary basis, with social workers being perhaps one of a number of professionals involved in an assessment.

We recognise that social work educators frequently supplement recommended reading in textbooks with a range of matter, including sections of other textbooks and journal articles. To some extent, this approach can help overcome the limitations of an individual textbook. However, this does not overcome the need for careful selection of recommended textbooks in the first place. Educators who have some responsibility for teaching social work assessment may find the detailed critiques for each textbooks included in this study in Appendices 1 and 2 to be a useful resource in selecting textbooks. We nevertheless acknowledge that these summaries are somewhat subjective, and that all of the reviewed textbooks had some merits. Alternatively, the framework adopted in these appendices may provide educators with a process for systematically evaluating other textbooks with content on assessment.

For other readers of this review, including social work students, practitioners and service users and carers, a key message is that what are considered the key issues in, and skills required for, social work assessment are contested. Assessment is a complex task and reading one textbook on the subject is unlikely to lead, on its own, to developing expert skills in the assessment process. This is one of the reasons why social work students spend a considerable part of their studies undertaking supervised practice learning in agency settings. Nevertheless, readers who are wanting to learn more about assessment practice may find the information in Appendices 1 and 2 helpful in identifying textbooks that match some of their learning needs.

Finally, for those who aspire to write social work textbooks, there are a number of issues that this study has highlighted. These include the need to define key terms such as assessment, to be explicit about the intended audience and have a clear understanding of their likely learning needs, as well as to be explicit about the theoretical and evidence bases that underpin the material presented. Authors also need to give careful consideration to whether pedagogical aids, such as case studies, learning exercises and recommendations for further reading, might enhance the potential for their textbook to facilitate learning, and if so, how.

Key points
- This study was restricted to textbooks published between 1994 and 2003 that included one or more chapters on assessment.
- The inclusion of textbooks in this sample does not imply any judgement as to their suitability for teaching UK students about social work assessment.
- There was considerable variety between textbooks as to the extent of detail and topics covered in relation to assessment.
- Changes in emphasis over time and differences in emphasis between textbooks published in the UK and North America were found.
- Several books and articles, which were out of the scope for this study, may well provide highly relevant content on some aspects of assessment, for example, service user and carer perspectives and multidisciplinary assessment.
- Readers are encouraged to use Appendices 1 and 2 of this review to identify textbooks that meet their needs in relation to assessment or to use this framework to critically analyse content in other textbooks on assessment.

Study 2: assessment frameworks

3.1 Introduction

It is often claimed that busy social workers do not have time to read the empirical literature,[237] and even if they did, many social workers have reportedly no access to departmental libraries or to professional journals through their workplace.[238] Consequently, it is not surprising that research evidence has been found to be rarely used to underpin decision making by social workers concerning interventions with their clients.[239] For example, when asked to make an assessment and recommendations for intervention based on a written scenario, social workers in both Canada and Israel were unlikely to claim empirical studies as the basis for their recommendations.[240]

An alternative model of research utilisation, which places less emphasis on individual practitioners keeping abreast of research and applying it to their practice, is to embed research findings in systems and processes of social work, such as standards, policies, procedures, frameworks and tools.[241] Hence, the emergence of evidence-based practice has sometimes resulted in increasing systemisation of professional practice through the issuing of practice guidance.[242] In respect of assessment, this has occurred in such diverse fields as child protection,[243] medical insurance[244] and environmental law.[245] Such guidance, sometimes known as assessment frameworks, is claimed to have the potential to encourage both effective outcomes for clients and effective interactions with them.[246]

As well as the potential to provide guidance that is empirically grounded, assessment frameworks may limit the effect of poor conceptual skills among assessors. For example, it is has been proposed that child protection workers rarely theorise in an informed or explicit manner.[247] In the absence of a formalised assessment framework, assessors may develop their own set of assessment objectives that they can readily articulate. However, those who are more uncertain about their framework will often be less clear as to their purpose, and may indicate weak conceptual skills in relation to the assessment process.[248]

The lack of a widely accepted assessment framework may also result in an absence of consensus as to the expectations of other stakeholders in the assessment process. Assessment frameworks may suggest the domains that should be expected to be considered in an assessment. In the absence of explicit expectations, assessors may fail to include discussion of topics that might otherwise be regarded as core information. For example, an analysis of expert reports submitted by expert witnessed in 20 cases of legal proceedings for alleged child sexual abuse in Sweden found that the written reports varied between two and 69 pages in length. Furthermore, there seemed to be no consensus as to whether such reports should include information about issues such as family and peer relations, emotional reactions in relation to the disclosure of abuse, psychological symptoms, behavioural disturbances, developmental ability and contact with other health professionals.[249]

It is perhaps unsurprising that assessment frameworks are sometimes proposed as the basis for training students and practitioners in particular forms of assessment.[250] Nevertheless, getting the best out of an assessment framework may necessitate novice users seeking out expert advice or supervision. As one of the developers of the Darlington Family Assessment System (DFAS) notes:

> For clinicians learning to use the DFAS, where cases are very complex and formulation difficult, or where risks for the wellbeing of family members are causing concern, then further advice should be sought from more experienced or specialized professionals.... Good supervision is essential, and should aim to enhance the conceptual skills of relating theory to practice; the technical skills of family interviewing; and be sensitive to the personal life experiences of novice therapists insofar as this affects their clinical work. Good supervision should help novice clinicians from what ever profession consider possible psychiatric diagnoses (such as ADHD, or psychotic conditions) and the need for additional specialist advice or multi-professional work in complex cases.[251]

Other writers are somewhat less optimistic about the potential of assessment frameworks to improve assessment practice. For example, it has been contended that explicit guidelines may result in assessment reports in which the basis for recommendations are more transparent or verifiable. However, greater transparency will not necessarily change the substance of assessors' recommendations.[252] Furthermore, even if there are standards for what sort of information they should collect, the weight that assessors give some information may vary considerably and there is no guarantee that they will include so-called essential details.[253] Thus, within the one agency, the likelihood of a determination of need for service may be dependent on which assessor has been allocated to a case.[254] Finally, just because assessment guidelines have been produced, it should not be assumed that workers are familiar with them. Despite the publication of Practice Guidance to accompany promulgation of the Carers (Recognition and Services) Act 1995, a study of Welsh care managers found that few were aware of its existence more than a year after the Act had taken effect. Consequently, many assessments were being conducted by assessors who were oblivious of the parameters and key principles of the assessment process in respect of carers.[255]

Whereas the above criticisms are concerned with implementation, contentions have been made about the "theory-neutral stance"[256] of some assessment tools and guidelines that are widely used in the UK. For example, it has been proposed that many widely used

> published government guides to assessment ... have not employed a theoretical framework which could evaluate and integrate the various professions, disciplines and perspectives which are involved.[257]

This study will involve an examination of a sample of assessment frameworks currently being used in social work and social care in the UK in order to explore the potential of assessment frameworks to educate students and workers about the assessment process more generally than in relation to the specific population for which it was designed.

Key points

- Social workers are often unable to read original accounts of empirical research.
- One way of encouraging research utilisation is to embed research findings in systems and processes of social work, such as standards, policies, procedures, frameworks and tools.
- An absence of an accepted assessment framework can lead to wide variations in how assessments occur and are reported.

- Assessment frameworks have been proposed as effective tools in teaching about assessment.
- The development of assessment frameworks alone is unlikely to be sufficient to ensure good assessment practice.

3.1.1 What is an assessment framework?

'Protocols', 'guidelines', 'standards' and 'policy guidelines' are terms that are often used interchangeably.[258] These have similar aims, that is, to ensure that clients with the same needs receive a similar service irrespective of the individual professional they have contact with. Moreover, it is often envisaged that such guidance to professionals will be evidence-based, and/or take into account policy initiatives and legislative requirements. What differentiates an assessment framework from being mere guidance is the inclusion of an explicit theoretical or conceptual underpinning. Documents that have been proposed as assessment frameworks vary in length, from journal articles of a few pages to extensive series of monographs. While some assessment frameworks are stand-alone documents, others are incorporated into broader frameworks for services with particular client groups.

An assessment framework should provide guidance on the domains or concepts that an assessment should consider.[259] These may relate primarily to the individual who is being assessed[260] or may go beyond the domain of service users to consider also the type of organisational unit that is providing services to clients and the resources of the service delivery system (human, technological, information and financial),[261] and thus may aim to reshape services.[262] For example, a suggested framework for assessing the needs of carers might consider:

1. quality of life for the person for whom they care
2. quality of life for the carer
3. managing the caring role
4. service process outcomes.[263]

While the identification of domains might guide the structure of an assessment report, "frameworks are really only aide-memoires, or organising principles"[264] for effective practice. Importantly, an assessment framework is not the same as the assessment tools or data collection instruments used to collect the information on which the assessment is based. Nevertheless, tools may be developed to facilitate assessment within a particular framework[265] or frameworks may identify a range of possible assessment tools from which assessors may select those most appropriate in a particular situation. Such tools may "provide a helpful adjunct"[266] rather than replace a detailed assessment process.

One further issue for consideration is whether an assessment framework needs to define itself as a 'framework'. For example, the Darlington Family Assessment System (DFAS) is arguably an assessment framework, despite the absence of the word 'framework' from its title. It has a conceptual basis that sets out the parameters for assessment and guidelines for practitioners. It also includes rating scales and interview schedules that facilitate exploration of the specific domains identified in the conceptual framework, but notes the importance of "matching the choice of assessment to the situation, so that methods are appropriate for the purpose, acceptable to clients, efficient and effective".[267]

Key points
- An assessment framework has an explicit theoretical or conceptual underpinning.
- Documents that have been proposed as assessment frameworks vary in length, from a few pages to lengthy monographs.
- An assessment framework should provide guidance on the domains or concepts that should be considered in an assessment, but not necessarily the data collection tools to collect this information.

3.2 Method

3.2.1 Criteria for inclusion

Recognising that there is no standard definition for the term 'assessment framework', this study sought to identify assessment frameworks that were:

- primarily comprised of documentation that proposed a conceptual, philosophical and/or theoretical basis to assessment practice

- not primarily a data collection tool or instructions for the completion of such, although such tools may be included in a broader assessment framework
- developed for assessing social work and social care clients in the UK
- developed for national rather than local use
- readily available over the Internet at no cost to potential users
- currently recommended for use with specific populations and
- not known to have been superseded.

A further consideration, given that the overwhelming majority of UK social workers are employed in statutory settings, was that selected frameworks are likely to be used in statutory social work settings. Such frameworks are likely to be among the most widely utilised, and the ones that social work students and new practitioners might be most expected to be familiar with.

3.2.2 Identification of sample frameworks

Having determined the sample criteria, the process of identifying potential frameworks involved identifying frameworks the authors were already familiar with, asking colleagues for details of assessment frameworks in their fields of practice, and searching the Internet to find references to 'assessment frameworks'.

Where multiple frameworks were identified relating to ostensibly the same client group, only one framework was selected. As the *Framework for the assessment of children in need and their families* is the most widely developed and used assessment framework in the UK, inclusion of this framework in the sample was considered essential. Other frameworks were selected on the basis of having been developed for use with contrasting client groups, and where possible we sought frameworks produced by a diverse range of organisations.

The documents containing the four assessment frameworks that were reviewed for this study were:

- *Framework for the assessment of children in need and their families*[268]
- *A practitioner's guide to carers' assessments under the Carers and Disabled Children Act 2000*[269]

- *Integrated care for drug users: Integration principles and practice*[270] and
- *National service framework for older people.*[271]

The first two of these represent stand-alone assessment frameworks, whereas the latter two are frameworks for service delivery with particular populations that include an assessment framework. While *Integrated care for drug users* was produced by the Scottish Executive, the Department of Health published each of the other frameworks examined for this study.

3.2.3 Analysis framework

A standardised proforma was developed for analysis of the content of each of the selected assessment frameworks. This was adapted from the proformas previously developed to analyse the content on assessment in textbooks. The initial proforma was trialled and then modified as additional categories emerged that had not been anticipated but that were potentially relevant. The proforma collected data on the following categories:

- framework
- publisher
- date of publication
- related publications
- intention of framework
- intended audience
- number of pages
- definitions of assessment
- timing of assessment
- theoretical underpinnings
- the assessment process
- information obtained during the assessment process
- risk assessment
- multidisciplinary assessment
- involvement of users and carers in the process
- user and carer perspectives of the assessment process
- evidence bases

- inclusion of case studies
- anti-discriminatory/anti-oppressive practice
- languages other than English and use of interpreters
- legislation/legal frameworks
- organisational and resource issues
- comprehensiveness
- recommended further reading.

The completed proformas for the selected assessment frameworks can be found in Appendix 4.

3.3 Findings

A singular notion of an assessment framework was not found in the four documents reviewed in respect of content (level of details and topics), expectations of prior knowledge by the intended readership, and intentions. Whereas the authors of *A practitioner's guide to carers' assessments* suggests that:

> This guide is designed to be a good practice tool for practitioners carrying out carers' assessments.[272]

the emphasis of the *Framework for the assessment of children in need and their families* is more of a "conceptual map"[273] than a how-to-do-it guide:

> The Guidance is not a practice manual. It does not set out step-by-step procedures to be followed: rather it sets out a framework which should be adapted and used to suit individual circumstances.[274]

Key point
- There was no agreement between the four documents reviewed in respect of level of details and topics covered; that is, there was no agreement as to what constitutes an assessment framework.

3.3.1 Audience

The frameworks that met the inclusion criteria for this study were not all aimed at the same audience. Two of the frameworks (the *Framework for the assessment of children in need and their families* and *Integrated care for drug users*) were aimed at a wide range of professional groupings who may have some involvement in the assessment process but made few assumptions about the knowledge levels of their disparate readerships. These documents provided far more introductory information about assessment and of the needs of the target population. One of these included the only definition of assessment. In many ways, these two frameworks included content that in both scope and extent made them not dissimilar from some of the introductory textbooks reviewed in the previous study (see Chapter 2). The remaining two frameworks (*A practitioner's guide to carers' assessments* and the *National service framework for older people*) were also aimed at a range of professional groups involved in assessment but assumed substantial expertise in both assessment practice and in working with the target population.

Key point
- Assessment frameworks make differing assumptions about readers' levels of knowledge of assessment.

3.3.2 What is assessment?

Only one of the frameworks actually defined assessment. This was the *Framework for the assessment of children in need and their families*, and draws heavily on the work of Compton and Galaway:

Assessment is the first stage in helping a vulnerable child and his or her family, its purpose to contribute to the understanding necessary for appropriate planning and action. Assessment has several phases which overlap and lead into planning, action and review:

- clarification of source of referral and reason
- acquisition of information
- exploring facts and feelings
- giving meaning to the situation which distinguishes the child and

family's understanding and feelings from those of the professionals

- reaching an understanding of what is happening, problems, strengths and difficulties, and the impact on the child (with the family wherever possible)
- drawing up an analysis of the needs of the child and parenting capacity within their family and community context as a basis for formulating a plan.[275]

Although not actually defining assessment, two other frameworks certainly hint at a definition by discussing the purpose. For example, *Integrated care for drug users* contends that:

> The purpose of assessment is to identify the needs and aspirations of the individual in order to inform decisions about treatment, care and support for drug users. It usually takes the form of one-to-one discussions between the staff member and the individual. If the assessment process is working effectively, the individual should be a full participant and understand and agree the goals of treatment, care and support.[276]

While the purpose of assessment just described is particularly focused on the needs of service users, *A practitioner's guide to carers' assessments* places greater emphasis on the capacity of service providers to meet the needs of service users and carers:

> A carers' assessment under the Carers and Disabled Children Act 2000 is carried out at the request of the carer in order:
>
> - to determine whether the carer is eligible for support
> - to determine the support needs of the carer (ie what will help the carer in their caring role and help them to maintain their own health and well-being
> - to see if those needs can be met by social or other services.[277]

In each of the four frameworks, determining a need for services was underpinned by an ethos in which the assessment process was concerned with the identification and management of risk. For example, *Integrated care for drug users* notes that assessment of risk is a core aspect of assessment, both in relation to establishing access to services and priority on any waiting lists for services. The identification of risk, however, meant different things in relation to the disparate target groups of the various assessment frameworks. While both the *Framework for the assessment of children in need and their families* and the *National service framework for older people* seek to identify persons who are perceived to be 'vulnerable' so that measures can be taken to reduce or avoid the potential for significant harm, in respect of older persons, the role of assessments is also to promote independence where possible by seeking to prevent deterioration and manage crises. In respect of carers, *A practitioner's guide to carers' assessments* considers risk in relation to the sustainability of the caring role, in other words, whether it is at risk of breaking down.

With the exception of the *National service framework for older people*, assessment was considered by the various frameworks to occur on an ongoing basis, while taking care not to be too repetitive or intrusive. This approach recognises that the needs of clients change over time, particularly after critical events.

Key points
- The purpose of an assessment may be defined in respect of the needs of either service users or service providers.
- A key purpose in undertaking assessments in all frameworks was the identification and management of risk.
- Three of the four frameworks in this study considered assessment to occur on an ongoing basis rather than at a single point of time.

3.3.3 The assessment process

Although the purpose of assessment frameworks is principally to provide practice guidance, a reasonable expectation may be that such guidance has an explicit theoretical underpinning. However, only the *Framework for the assessment of children in need and their families* discusses the need to underpin practice with theory, but it does not identify specific theories. Furthermore, it notes other bases for practice:

Each professional discipline derives its knowledge from a particular theoretical base, related research findings and accumulated practice wisdom and experience. Social work practice, however, differs in that it derives its knowledge base from theory and research in many different disciplines. Practice is also based on policies laid down in legislation and government guidance. It is essential that practitioners and their managers ensure that practice and its supervision are grounded in the most up to date knowledge and that they make the best use of the resources described in the practice guidance as well as other critical materials including:

- relevant research findings
- national and local statistical data
- national policy and practice guidance
- Social Services Inspectorate Inspection Standards
- government and local inspection, audit and performance assessment reports
- lessons learnt from national and local inquiries and reviews of cases of child maltreatment.[278]

Single Shared Assessment, which utilises a person-centred planning approach, is advocated in both *Integrated care for drug users* and the *National service framework for older people*. However, while the former introduces these concepts to the reader and assumes no prior familiarity with these ideas, these concepts are not explained in the latter. No explicit theoretical underpinning is apparent in *A practitioner's guide to carers' assessments*, with the stated underpinnings of this guide being the Carers and Disabled Children Act 2000.

Although explicit discussion of theoretical underpinnings would seem somewhat optional in an assessment framework, explicit expectations about the assessment process are not. All of the frameworks included lists of domains that must be included, or at least considered for inclusion, in an assessment. Structured recording instruments, and accompanying volumes providing details of suggested tools, are available for the *Framework for the assessment of children in need and their families*[279] and *Integrated care for drug users*,[280] but ultimately for all of the reviewed frameworks, a high degree of professional skill is expected, and this includes skills in selecting appropriate measures. The extent of information and range of domains covered may also be affected by the level of assessment undertaken, with the *Framework for the assessment of children in need and their families* outlining both 'initial' and 'core' assessment, and *Integrated care for drug users* proposing 'simple', 'comprehensive' and 'specialist' assessment for use in differing circumstances.

In addition to outlining the domains that should be covered in an assessment, each of the frameworks outlines a range of expectations about assessors and their conduct of assessments. These may include prescriptive statements about timeframes for interviews, minimum requirements for information provision, content of an assessment report, and issues around consent, confidentiality and disclosure. All of the frameworks include expectations that an assessment may be multidisciplinary in nature. While the *Framework for the assessment of children in need and their families* was most explicit in respect of the particular responsibilities of different agencies and disciplines, the general ethos of the frameworks was that (a) a range of expert opinions may be required, and (b) these should be obtained in a coordinated and planned way, seeking to avoid the situation of service users and carers having to provide the same information on multiple occasions.

Key points
- There is little, if any, discussion of the theoretical underpinnings of the assessment process in assessment frameworks.
- Each of the frameworks outlines a range of expectations about assessors and their conduct of assessments, such as timeframes for interviews, minimum requirements for information provision, content of an assessment report, and issues around consent, confidentiality and disclosure.
- All of the frameworks include lists of domains that must be included, or at least considered for inclusion, in an assessment.
- Structured recording instruments, and accompanying volumes providing details of suggested tools, are available for some assessment frameworks.
- A common expectation was that assessments may be multidisciplinary in nature.

3.3.4 Involvement of service users and carers in the assessment process

The involvement of service users and carers is considered integral to the assessment process in all of the frameworks reviewed. Assessment should be about determining the client's needs, but should not be a process that is 'done to' people. In respect of carer assessments, the practice guidance notes:

- The assessment is not a test for the carer. It should not be prescriptive but recognise the carers' knowledge and expertise.
- The assessment should listen to what carers are saying and offer an opportunity for private discussion so the carer can be candid.
- It should not be a bureaucratic process based on ticking boxes. It must focus on the outcomes the carer would want to see to help them in their caring role and maintain their health and well-being. [281]

Furthermore, care should be taken to ensure that the needs of the person who is being assessed are considered paramount, and not allowed to be lost in the myriad of needs of other family members, such as parents, siblings or carers. Thus, for example, the focus of an assessment of children should be the child, and the process child-centred, with the perspective of the child given prominence. Similarly, assessments of carers should be carer-centred, with carers being entitled to have their own assessment independent of any assessments of the person for whom they are caring.

While working in partnership with service users and carers is recommended, it is, nevertheless, recognised that some assessments may need to be conducted when this working arrangement is not possible. As the *Framework for the assessment of children in need and their families* notes:

Generally, all these phases of the assessment process should be undertaken in partnership with the child and key family members, and with their agreement. This includes finalising the plan of action. There may be exceptions when there are concerns that a child is suffering or may be suffering significant harm. [282]

Although each of the frameworks reviewed for this study stressed the importance of a client-centred approach, only *Integrated care for drug users* included feedback from service users about their experiences of being assessed. This information came from focus groups, which were conducted as part of the process of developing the framework.

Key points
- The involvement of service users and carers is considered integral to the assessment process in all of the frameworks reviewed.
- Assessment should be about determining the client's needs, but should not be a process that is 'done to' people.
- Only one assessment framework includes feedback from service users about the experience of being assessed.

3.3.5 Legislation and policy contexts

The reviewed frameworks were all published by government agencies and reflect current policy objectives. For example, the *National service framework for older people*:

> ... is the first ever comprehensive strategy to ensure fair, high quality, integrated health and social care services for older people. It is a 10 year programme of action linking services to support independence and promote good health, specialised services for key conditions, and culture change so that all older people and their carers are always treated with respect, dignity and fairness.[283]

Two of the frameworks reviewed were explicitly framed in relation to specific legislation: *A practitioner's guide to carer's assessments under the 2000 Carers and Disabled Childrens Act*, which even refers to legislation in the name of the framework. Nevertheless, this framework also mentions other legislation and the fact that assessors may also need to take into account the requirements of other guidance such as the *Framework for the assessment of children and need and their families*, a framework which in turn is informed by legislative requirements:

> The Guidance describes the Assessment Framework and the Government's expectations of how it will be used. It reflects the

principles contained within the United Nations Convention on the Rights of the Child, ratified by the UK government in 1991 and the Human Rights Act 1998. In addition, it takes account of relevant legislation at the time of publication, but is particularly informed by the requirements of the Children Act 1989, which provides a comprehensive framework for the care and protection of children.[284]

The remaining two frameworks, however, make only brief mentions of legislation and/or the legal context in which assessments occur. It should be noted, however, that even where legislation was mentioned, a working knowledge of the relevant legislation seemed to be assumed, as it was not provided.

Key points
- Assessment frameworks published by government agencies reflect current policy objectives.
- Frameworks may or may not be framed explicitly in relation to specific legislation.

3.3.6 Anti-discriminatory and anti-oppressive practice

The terms 'anti-discriminatory' and 'anti-oppressive' practice are not specifically mentioned in the reviewed frameworks. However, three of them did discuss the need for assessment practice that takes into account diversity and addresses disadvantage and discrimination. Standard One in the *National service framework for older people* is titled 'Rooting out age discrimination'. In relation to assessment specifically, the need to recognise individual needs, including gender, cultural and religious differences, is mentioned. Likewise, the *Framework for the assessment of children and need and their families* includes a section on 'Inclusive practice'. Taking a different approach, the *A practitioner's guide to carers' assessments* does not have a separate section nor use the terms 'anti-discriminatory' and 'anti-oppressive' practice, but notes the need to ensure that carers from black and minority ethnic backgrounds are not discriminated against. For example, it suggests that one of the questions that assessors should consider in relation to sustainability of the caring role is: "How appropriate is the role for someone of the carer's culture, religion, gender?".[285]

Only two the frameworks reviewed made mention of clients or carers for whom English is not their first language, and both also discussed communicating with clients or carers with a disability that may require use of British Sign Language, Braille or some other alternative to standard formats of information provision. While the *National service framework for older people* only discusses this in relation to the provision of information, the *Framework for the assessment of children in need and their families* raises the issue of language skills in relation to the assessment process. In particular, it notes that: "Additional specialist help may be necessary if the child's first language is not English".[286]

Key points

- Although seeking to overcome discrimination is an objective of the assessment frameworks reviewed for this study, the terms 'anti-discriminatory' and 'anti-oppressive' practice are not specifically mentioned.
- The needs of clients who speak a language other than English, including British Sign Language, were mentioned in only two frameworks.

3.3.7 Evidence bases

Three of the frameworks were extensively referenced. The exception was *A practitioner's guide to carers' assessments*, in which the reader is informed that: "Research by The Social and Policy Research Unit at York University (SPRU) has identified a range of outcomes carers may see as desirable",[287] but other than involving discussions between researchers and carers, it is unclear how such evidence was collected.

In stark contrast, the *National service framework for older people* included a typology of evidence, with 11 possible categories. Alongside each in-text reference, the type of evidence is denoted according to the key in Table 3.

Table 3: Typology of evidence in the *National service framework for older people*[288]

Evidence from research and other professional literature	
A1	Systematic reviews that include at least one Randomised Controlled Trial (RCT) (e.g. systematic reviews from Cochrane or Centre for Reviews and Dissemination)
A2	Other systematic and high quality reviews which synthesise references
B1	Individual RCTs
B2	Individual non-randomised, experimental/intervention studies
B3	Individual well-designed non-experimental studies, controlled statistically if appropriate. Includes studies using case control; longitudinal, cohort, matched pairs, or cross-sectional random sample methodologies; and well-designed qualitative studies; and well-designed analytical studies, including secondary analysis
C1	Descriptive and other research or evaluation not in B (e.g. convenience samples)
C2	Case studies and examples of good practice
D	Summary review articles and discussions of relevant literature and conference proceedings not otherwise classified
Evidence from expert opinion	
P	Professional opinion based on clinical evidence or reports of committees
U	User opinion from Older People's Reference Group or similar
C	Carer opinion from Carer's Focus Group or similar

A similar process was adopted in *Integrated care for drug users*, with evidence being denoted as being systematic reviews (Type 1), narrative reviews (Type 2), primary research studies (Type 3), user consultations (Type 4) and working groups and other consultations of the Effective Interventions Unit (Type 5).

Although the *Framework for the assessment of children in need and their families* was extensively referenced, the referencing was more akin to that found in textbooks, in which the evidence bases are not explicitly typologised each time they are referred to. However, it places greater emphasis on encouraging assessors to adopt an evidence-based approach to their practice:

Practice is expected to be evidence-based, by which it is meant that practitioners:

- use knowledge critically from research and practice about the needs of children and families and the outcomes of services and interventions to inform their assessment and planning
- record and update information systematically, distinguishing between sources of information, for example direct observation, other agency records or interviews with family members
- valuate continuously whether the intervention is effective in responding to the needs of an individual child and family and modifying their interventions accordingly
- evaluate rigorously the information, processes and outcomes from the practitioner's own interventions to develop practice wisdom.[289]

Key points
- Each of the assessment frameworks stresses the expectation that practice is clearly grounded in evidence.
- In contrast to the textbooks in the previous study (see Chapter 2), there is more explicit discussion of research evidence used to underpin the frameworks. Two assessment frameworks typologise references into categories of evidence.

3.3.8 Pedagogy

Unlike several of the textbooks in the previous study (see Chapter 2), none of the frameworks included learning exercises to facilitate learning. Furthermore, only two frameworks included case examples that demonstrated how theory might be implemented in practice. *A practitioner's guide to carers' assessments* includes a number of case studies of service users and carers, while *Integrated care for drug users* includes case studies that demonstrate (a) processes from a client perspective, and (b) good agency practice.

Two of the frameworks, the *Framework for the assessment of children in need and their families* and *Integrated care for drug users*, included numerous recommendations in the text for further reading, the latter primarily for web-based materials. Although the *National service framework for older people* makes no specific recommendations for further reading, a lengthy bibliography is included. Neither recommendations for further reading nor a bibliography are included in *A practitioner's guide to carers' assessments*.

Key points
- Use of pedagogical aids in the assessment frameworks to facilitate learning was limited.
- Two frameworks include case studies of service users and two include recommendations for further reading.

3.4 Discussion

This study sought to examine the extent to which assessment frameworks can be used to facilitate learning about assessment by social work and social care students and professionals. We found considerable variety in the frameworks that we reviewed in respect of the extent of detail and topics covered. While the *Framework for the assessment of children in need and their families* and *Integrated care for drug users* provided as much, if not more, detail on the assessment process than many of the textbooks reviewed in the previous study, frameworks such as the *National service framework for older people* provided little of this information, assuming its readership were already skilled assessors. It is therefore not possible to make a generalised statement about the extent to which assessment frameworks can teach students and professionals about the assessment process. Rather, if assessment frameworks are to be used to teach more generally about assessment, care in the selection of these will be required.

For each of the assessment frameworks reviewed for this study, the identification and management of risk was a key purpose of the assessment process for service providers, although the motivation for service users to participate may be due more to a desire to gain access to specific services. Another common theme across the frameworks was the expectation that an assessment may require input from a range of agencies or disciplines. However, there was very little discussion about the theoretical underpinnings of the assessment process in any of the documents we reviewed. Even if the legislative basis for assessment was mentioned, a working knowledge of the relevant legislation seemed to be assumed, as it was not provided. Furthermore, although the involvement of service users and carers was considered integral to the assessment process in all of the reviewed frameworks, only one included any input from service users about the experience of being assessed.

Even with one of the seemingly more comprehensive assessment frameworks, such as the *Framework for the assessment of children in need and their families*, it would be a mistake to assume that students or practitioners will become expert assessors simply by following the printed practice guidance. There is a further assumption that skilled assessors are able to articulate the reasoning for their actions, despite evidence that this may not apply to many experienced practitioners.[290] Consequently, assessment frameworks can readily be used as mechanistic checklists rather than providing conceptual guidance[291] and inexperienced staff may use the proforma recording forms for reporting assessments as data collection tools, even though this was not what they were designed for:

> … there is a danger the Assessment Framework will become form-led and interpreted merely as yet another procedure to follow when workers do not have the opportunity to familiarize themselves with and work to the principles. In this situation, the focus becomes information-gathering. Making sense of the information becomes secondary and the focus on both identifying and meeting the needs of the child is lost.[292]

Consequently, if frameworks are being used to provide training about assessment in social work and related settings, we would echo previous recommendations that the provision of professional supervision is essential for the effective implementation of assessment frameworks.[293] Good supervision also has the potential to make inroads against claims that many professionals are unclear as to their roles and responsibilities in relation to frameworks, or may not even know about them.[294] However, we recognise the temptation within a bureaucracy for what is perceived as 'good practice' to be uncritically aligned with worker compliance to bureaucratic requirements:

> Children continue to die at the hands of their parents. The response still seems to be to create more procedures and more guidelines. The sheer scale and compass of these documents makes it almost inevitable that the social worker with a dead child on her caseload will have failed in some aspect of her highly regulated practice. Simply adding new procedures in the wake of yet another tragedy merely compounds the problem. This pushes the social worker into ever more defensive forms of practice which make her less sensitive to the people involved and more concerned with the procedures which govern her behaviour. Once the powers-that-be have written the rules and established the routines, all that the wary social worker and her supervisor have to do if blame is to be avoided is to 'go by the book'. Responsibility for failures cannot be attached to the worker if she behaved correctly and ensured that all that should be done was done. 'Defensive' social work may not be effective but it can be 'right'.[295]

Despite the fact that the assessment frameworks reviewed for this study represent official government policies, with some statutory requirements for use of the *Framework for the assessment of children in need and their families* in England and Wales, official status does not ensure good practice. Indeed, there are numerous criticisms of this framework, including that much of the evidence underpinning the framework for children in need is problematic.[296] Similar criticisms have also been made in relation to the *National service framework for older people.*[297] Furthermore, as with any policy document, the extent to which practice occurs as intended is questionable[298] and variations between organisations or regions may be anticipated.[299] In respect of the *Framework for the assessment of children in need and their families*, it has been suggested that the effectiveness of the framework in improving assessment practice would appear highly dependent on local practices, and in some places it would seem that the framework has not been implemented as envisaged.[300] The need for training of senior managers, not just direct service staff, has been identified,[301] as has the need to develop better inter-agency working arrangements.[302]

Most of the reviewed frameworks had one or more accompanying documents that were identified in the process of conducting this study, especially for the *Framework for the assessment of children in need and their families*.[303] These may provide more comprehensive guidance than the key framework document. For example, it has been suggested that the Practice Guidance accompanying this framework provides specific guidance in relation to children from black and minority ethnic communities, and disabled children, but that accompanying documents are far less widely distributed than the framework document itself.[304] Hence, the approach taken in this study, of focusing primarily on the framework documents themselves, reflects a potentially common pattern of utilisation by the practitioners at which they are aimed.

Notwithstanding the limitations identified in respect of the selected assessment frameworks and our methodology, the key question for this study is that of transferability, that is, to what extent can assessment frameworks facilitate learning on assessment that is transferable to other settings or populations? Undoubtedly, they form a useful resource, often complementing textbooks. Clearly, the principles underpinning much of the guidance provided in the various frameworks is often applicable in settings and with population groups other than that for which it was originally envisaged. However, as each framework has been developed to assist in the assessment of specific groups, transferability is not something that the framework documents highlight. Rather, it tends to be left to the reader to apply these principles to assessments beyond the scope of the particular framework documents.

We recognise that many social work educators are increasingly feeling pressured to teach students to use assessment frameworks. Given that assessment frameworks have been and are being developed for a wide range of practice situations, this expectation is not unreasonable. Nevertheless, although assessment frameworks tend towards providing highly practical advice, educators need to ensure that students are also provided with opportunities to learn about issues that may not be covered well in the frameworks, for example theoretical perspectives and the experiences of service users in the assessment process. Social work educators may find the analyses of the assessment frameworks reviewed for this study in Appendix 4 provide a method for critically analysing frameworks they are seeking to include in their teaching. These analyses may also assist educators in identifying issues they will need to consider in order to look beyond the frameworks as a source of knowledge for students.

For other readers of this review, including social work students, practitioners and service users and carers, it is important to recognise that while assessment frameworks may make explicit some expectations about the assessment process, they may also be based on an implicit assumption that professionals conducting assessments already have some baseline knowledge of the process. Using the headings in Appendix 4 as a tool may help identify some aspects of the assessment process about which knowledge may be needed but not provided in a particular framework document. For student readers, an important message is that reading an assessment framework alone will not make one an expert in assessment. Our own experience is that assessment is a very complex task, and that it is not only necessary to learn what is in an assessment framework, but also to learn how to use it in practice. Supervised practice learning and supervised practice in the workplace are therefore an essential complement to assessment framework documents.

Finally, for those who are developing assessment frameworks or practice guidelines, it would seem important to be explicit as to what level of knowledge and skills are presupposed of those using these materials. Hence, recommendations for further reading, especially on topics where background knowledge is assumed, may well enhance the potential of an assessment framework as a tool for learning and teaching about assessment. Furthermore, although an assessment framework may be introduced with expectations of staff training and supervision to assist assessors in getting to grips with the requirements, this does not always happen in practice. Hence, the inclusion of case studies and learning exercises may be crucial in ensuring that an assessment framework can act as a tool for enhancing learning about assessment.

Key points

- As assessment frameworks vary considerably, it is not possible to make a generalised statement as to if and how they can be used to teach about the assessment process.
- The need to identify and manage risk is a key feature of each of the four frameworks reviewed for this study, as is an expectation that the assessment might involve a range of professionals and agencies.
- Only one framework discusses social work theories associated with assessment and only one includes service user and carer perspectives of the assessment process.
- It should not be assumed that students or practitioners will become expert assessors simply by following the printed practice guidance in assessment frameworks. In particular, the provision of professional supervision is essential for the effective implementation of assessment frameworks.
- Good practice does not necessarily equate with compliance to published practice guidance such as assessment frameworks.
- As each framework has been developed to assist in assessment of specific groups, the transferability of skills and knowledge to other contexts is not promoted by assessment framework documents.
- Readers are encouraged to use Appendix 4 of this review as a tool for critically analysing the content of assessment frameworks and to identify topics for which they would need to seek information from other sources.

4

Conclusion and recommendations

This report reviewed two types of publications to which a reader might turn when seeking information about the assessment process, namely textbooks and assessment frameworks. Both are widely read documents that have the potential to lead to significant changes in practice but there are some significant differences between the two as well as considerable variation between documents of the same type. To some extent, it would seem that textbooks and assessment frameworks complement each other rather than one being a substitute for the other.

No single definition or conceptualisation of assessment was readily apparent in either study, although the identification and management of risk emerged as a common purpose for assessment in the assessment frameworks. Moreover, a number of documents reviewed failed to indicate what the authors meant by the term 'assessment' per se. Absence of a definition seems more likely in documents that were aimed at a more advanced audience than beginning social work students or newly appointed unqualified workers. One of the differences between textbooks and assessment frameworks is that the former are more likely to include explicit discussion of theoretical underpinnings in relation to assessment, and the latter are more likely to include specific guidelines about how practice should be undertaken, and to have an expectation that assessments may involve a range of agencies and professions. However, numerous exceptions to such generalisations hold. For example, the *Framework for the assessment of children in need and their families* provides as weighty a discussion on theoretical matters as many textbooks. Conversely, some textbooks, especially the North American ones,[305] provide detailed assessment frameworks that can be adapted for use in several settings.

All of the frameworks, and 13 of the 16 textbooks, were written for audiences in the UK or particular countries therein. However, the extent to which these took account of current practice concerns varied considerably. Very few textbooks or assessment frameworks included content from service users or carers with regard to their perspective of being assessed or discussed issues in relation to conducting assessments with clients whose first language is other than English. Even among those documents developed for use in the UK, there was considerable variation in relation to the extent, if any, of mentions of anti-discriminatory/anti-oppressive practice, legislation, and involvement of service users and carers in the assessment process. Mentions of these concerns were scant to non-existent in the textbooks produced overseas.

The explicitness of the evidence bases that underpinned writing on assessment also varies greatly. Two of the frameworks typologised all forms of evidence cited, and the reader could readily identify what type of evidence was being used to support particular guidelines. None of the textbooks systematically typologised evidence it cited in this way. While some textbooks explicitly discussed research findings, often the only way for the reader to gain insight into what form of evidence was included in citations was to go back to the original source material itself.

An explanation for some of the differences identified between textbooks and assessment frameworks may well be due to their differing origins. Textbooks are commissioned and sold by commercial publishing houses and the guidance they provide is suggested as being applicable in a diverse range of settings, and with diverse populations, but having no official status. Moreover, pedagogical aids, such as recommendations for additional reading, learning exercises and case examples, were more likely to be found in textbooks. By way of contrast, the assessment frameworks reviewed for this study were produced by government agencies and had varying degrees of official status in relation to expectations as to their use in guiding assessment practice with particular populations within specific countries.

One difference between the function of a textbook and an assessment framework that this review has not yet touched on the role of such documents in the career projectory of their authors. Edited texts that have emanated from various social work departments[306] have played an important role in introducing new authors to publishing. Furthermore, although disregarded by the Research Assessment Exercises (RAE), which rates the quality of research in university departments across the UK, authorship of a well-regarded textbook can bring esteem that contributes to promotion or appointment to senior academic positions. The extent to which career ambitions affect the content of textbooks is unknown, as is the extent to which content is compromised by the need for publishers to meet their costs and hopefully make a profit from sales.

By way of contrast, the assessment frameworks reviewed for this study listed corporate authors rather than individuals, and were freely available at no cost to potential readers.

A final concern of this study concerned transferability of knowledge and there are a number of findings in relation to this. First, much of the guidance provided in the various frameworks is often applicable for assessing populations other than those for which it was originally envisaged, although it is left to the reader to apply these principles more broadly. Second, textbooks reflect the concerns of both the era and the national setting in which they are written. Although textbooks written outside the UK and those written some years ago might make valuable contributions in relation to several issues associated with assessment, they are likely to need contextualising through supplementary readings in either textbooks or assessment frameworks. Third, differing legal systems within the UK can limit the transferability of information in textbooks and assessment frameworks between England, Wales, Scotland and Northern Ireland in relation to legal frameworks and legislation.

All of the documents reviewed for this study had some shortcomings in respect of (a) the adequacy with which they covered key content areas and/or (b) inclusion of pedagogical devices to active learning. As the potential readership of information on assessment is, in the main, likely to be busy students or workers who do not have unlimited time for reading, it is important that what reading on assessment is recommended is most appropriate for a particular readership. While the findings pertaining to this review are likely to be of most interest to those educators who are deciding what books or frameworks they might use to promote learning and teaching about assessment to either students or practitioners, the approach taken in this study also provides a model for critically analysing and selecting learning materials for social work education more generally. This involved identifying (a) how assessment was conceptualised, (b) theoretical and evidence bases, (c) current practice concerns and determining the adequacy of information provided in relation to these, and (d) pedagogical aids to enhance learning. This approach could readily be adapted for reviewing learning resources for other aspects of the social work curriculum, and also for learning materials produced for cognate disciplines, such as the health sciences and education.

Key points

- Textbooks and assessment frameworks seem to complement each other rather than one being a substitute for the other.
- All of the documents reviewed for this study have some shortcomings in respect of (a) the adequacy with which they cover key content areas and/or (b) inclusion of pedagogical devices to active learning.
- No single definition or conceptualisation of assessment is readily apparent among either textbooks or assessment frameworks, although the identification and management of risk emerges as a common purpose for assessment in the assessment frameworks.
- Textbooks are more likely to include explicit discussion of theoretical underpinnings in relation to assessment, whereas assessment frameworks are more likely to include specific guidelines about how practice should be undertaken, and to have an expectation that assessments may involve a range of agencies and professions.
- Very few of the textbooks or assessment frameworks examined include content from service users or carers with regard to their perspective of being assessed or discussed issues in relation to conducting assessments with clients whose working language is other than English.
- The explicitness of the evidence bases that underpinned writing on assessment also varies greatly. Two assessment frameworks but no textbook typologise each piece of supporting evidence.
- Differences between textbooks and assessment frameworks may be due to their differing origins.

Taking the findings of this review further, we wish to conclude by making recommendations with the aim of developing critical development and use of textbooks and assessment frameworks. The first of these are aimed at all readers of textbooks and assessment frameworks, including students, practitioners, service users and educators. The second set of recommendations is aimed at social work educators who use these documents to facilitate learning. Finally, there are recommendations aimed at authors of textbooks and assessment frameworks.

4.1   Recommendations for all readers

- Readers need to be aware that legislative, policy and practice contexts are not static, and should not assume that textbooks and assessment frameworks that have been published for some time are an accurate reflection of current practice.
- Readers need to be particularly aware that some textbooks, especially those published overseas, reflect a rather different context for social work practice. On the other hand, such textbooks may offer useful insights, especially on topics poorly covered in local literature.
- Readers in the UK need to be aware that there will be some differences in legislation and organisation of practice between England, Wales, Scotland and Northern Ireland.
- Readers should not assume that they will develop expertise in assessment only by reading relevant textbooks and assessment frameworks. Attempting learning exercises contained in textbooks and assessment frameworks, discussion of concepts and practices in supervision, and ultimately attempting to put the theory into practice, are all further steps in becoming a skilled practitioner.

4.2   Recommendations for social work educators

- It is unlikely that reading textbooks or assessment frameworks alone will result in competent assessment practice. Students and inexperienced practitioners need opportunities to explore and develop the complex set of skill and knowledge requirements presented in textbooks and assessment frameworks, ideally in some form of supervised practice.
- Educators should have a clear rationale for recommending/requiring students/practitioners to read particular textbooks or assessment frameworks.
- Educators need to be aware of the limitations of the textbooks and assessment frameworks they recommend. In particular, an awareness is required of any changes in policy, legislation or expectations of practitioners that might result in some information contained in textbooks or assessment frameworks being outdated or superseded. It may be necessary to make such information known to students/practitioners

or recommend supplementary readings that are not subject to such constraints.

4.3 Recommendations for authors

- Be explicit as to who the intended audience is. It is acceptable to assume some prior knowledge of practice processes provided it is made clear that the textbook/assessment framework is not aiming to provide introductory knowledge to basic practice skills. Recommendations for alternative reading could be made for readers seeking out more introductory information on assessment.
- Define concepts such as assessment, for which there is no single definition.
- Include case studies and learning exercises to encourage more active learning.
- Explicitly discuss the theoretical and evidence bases that underpin the writing. Although these might be self-evident to the author, the reader should not have to second-guess what these might be.
- Recognise constraints such as word limits, and suggest recommended reading so that the audience can have some idea of where to read further on key topics.

Notes and references

[1] Department of Health, Department for Education and Employment and the Home Office (2000) *Framework for the assessment of children in need and their families*, London: The Stationery Office.

[2] The term 'social work educators' in this review refers to a range of persons involved in the provision of education and training to social work students and practitioners, including academic staff in universities and colleges, practice teachers and training officers in social work agencies.

[3] Crisp, B.R., Anderson, M.R., Orme, J. and Green Lister, P. (2003) *Knowledge review 1: Learning and teaching in social work education: Assessment*, London: Social Care Institute for Excellence.

[4] Department of Health et al (2000) *Framework for the assessment of children in need and their families*.

[5] Sheldon, B. and Chilvers, R. (2000) *Evidence-based social care: A study of prospects and problems*, Lyme Regis, Dorset: Russell House Publishing.

[6] Mertens, D.M. (1994) 'Training evaluators: unique skills and knowledge', *New Directions for Program Evaluation*, vol 62, pp 17-27.

[7] Maslow, W. (1981) 'American sociology as a "classist" discipline: an empirical inquiry into the treatment of Marx in the textbooks of North American sociology, 1890-1965', *Humanity and Society*, vol 5, pp 256-75, here p 257.

[8] Kramer, B.J., Pacourek, L. and Hovland-Scafe, C. (2003) 'Analysis of end-of-life content in social work textbooks', *Journal on Social Work Education*, vol 39, pp 299-320, here p 301.

[9] Ciborowski, J. (1995) 'Using textbooks with students who cannot read them', *Remedial and Special Education*, vol 16, pp 90-101, here p 100.

[10] Ornstein, A.C. (1994) 'The textbook-driven curriculum' *Peabody Journal of Education*, vol 69, no 3, pp 70-85.

[11] Agger, B. (1989) 'Do books write authors? a study of disciplinary hegemony', *Teaching Sociology*, vol 17, pp 365-9, here p 366.

[12] Strozier, A.L. (1997) 'Groupwork in social work education: what is being taught?', *Social Work with Groups*, vol 20, pp 65-77.

13 Strozier (1997) 'Groupwork in social work education', p 76.

14 Apple, M.W. and Christian-Smith, L.K. (1991) 'The politics of the textbook', in M.W. Apple and L.K. Christian-Smith (eds) *The politics of the textbook*, New York, NY: Routledge, p 2.

15 Apple and Christian-Smith (1991) 'The politics of the textbook'.

16 Wright, R.A., Sheridan, C. and del Carmen, R.V. (1997) 'Textbook adoption and other landmark decisions: the coverage of court cases in criminal justice textbooks, 1986 to 1995', *Journal of Criminal Justice Education*, vol 8, pp 145-54.

17 Stolley, K.S. and Hall, E.J. (1994) 'The presentation of abortion and adoption in marriage and family textbooks', *Family Relations*, vol 43, pp 267-73, here p 268.

18 Mertens (1994) 'Training evaluators'.

19 Koeske, G.F. (1994) 'Some recommendations for improving measurement validation in social work research', *Journal of Social Service Research*, vol 18, no 3/4, pp 43-72.

20 Ferrell, B., Virani, R. and Grant, M. (1999) 'Analysis of end-of-life content in nursing textbooks', *Oncology Nursing Forum*, vol 26, pp 869-76; Ferrell, B., Virani, R., Grant, M. and Juarez, G. (2000) 'Current reviews: analysis of palliative care content in nursing textbooks', *Journal of Palliative Care*, vol 16, pp 39-47.

21 Apple, M.W. (1991) 'The culture and commerce of the textbook', in M.W. Apple and L.K. Christian-Smith (eds) *The politics of the textbook*, New York, NY: Routledge.

22 Ornstein (1994) 'The textbook-driven curriculum', pp 70-1.

23 Carron, A.T., Lynn, J. and Keaney, P. (1999) 'End-of-life care in medical textbooks', *Annals of Internal Medicine*, vol 130, pp 82-6.

24 Apple (1991) 'The culture and commerce of the textbook'.

25 Hites, R.A. (2001) 'Evaluating environmental chemistry textbooks' *Environmental Science and Technology*, vol 35, pp 32A-38A.

26 Ferree, M. M. and Hall, E.J. (1996) 'Rethinking stratification from a feminist perspective: gender, race and class in mainstream textbooks', *American Sociological Review*, vol 61, pp 929-51.

27 Mertens (1994) 'Training evaluators'.

28 Wachholz, S. and Mullaly, B. (2000) 'The politics of the textbook: a content analysis of the coverage and treatment of feminist, radical and anti-racist social work scholarship in American introductory social work textbooks published between 1988 and 1997', *Journal of Progressive Human Services*, vol 11, no 2, pp 51-76.

29 Wachholz and Mullaly (2000) 'The politics of the textbook', p 68.

30 Carron et al (1999) 'End-of-life care'.

31 Rabow, M.W., Hardie, G.E., Fair, J.M. and McPhee, S.J. (2000) 'End-of-life care content in 50 textbooks from multiple specialties', *Journal of the American Medical Association*, vol 283, pp 771-8.

32 Kramer et al (2003) 'Analysis of end-of-life content'; Ruffolo, M., Sugamelle, M. and Taylor-Brown, S. (1994) 'Scapegoating of mothers: a study of mother-blaming in case studies introduced in core foundation social work practice textbooks', *Journal of Teaching in Social Work*, vol 10, no 1/2, pp 117-27.

33 Ruffolo et al (1994) 'Scapegoating of mothers'; Sleeter, C.E. and Grant, C.A. (1991) 'Race, class, gender and disability in current textbooks', in M.W. Apple and L.K. Christian-Smith (eds) *The politics of the textbook,* New York, NY: Routledge.

34 Cherlin, A.J. (1997) 'A reply to Glenn: what's most important in a family textbook?', *Family Relations*, vol 46, pp 209-11, here p 210.

35 Milner, J. and O'Byrne, P. (2002) *Assessment in social work* (2nd edn), Basingstoke: Macmillan, p 95.

36 Glenn, N.D. (1997) 'A critique of twenty family and marriage and the family textbooks', *Family Relations*, vol 46, pp 197-208.

37 Ornstein (1994) 'The textbook-driven curriculum', pp 71-2.

38 Altbach, P.G. (1991) 'Textbooks: the international dimension', in M.W. Apple and L.K. Christian-Smith (eds) *The politics of the textbook,* New York, NY: Routledge.

39 Maslow (1981) 'American sociology'.

40 Horner, R. (2003) *What is social work? Contexts and perspectives,* Exeter: Learning Matters; Parker, J. and Bradley, G. (2003) *Social work practice: Assessment, planning, intervention and review,* Exeter: Learning Matters.

41 Altbach (1991) 'Textbooks'.

42 Crisp et al (2003) *Knowledge review 1.*

43 Department of Health (2002) *Requirements for social work training,* London: Department of Health.

44 Department of Health, Social Services and Public Safety (2003) *Northern Ireland framework specification for the degree in social work,* Belfast: Department of Health, Social Services and Public Safety.

45 Scottish Executive (2003) *The framework for social work education in Scotland,* Edinburgh: The Stationery Office.

46 National Assembly for Wales (2003) *Requirements for an award of a degree in social work,* www.wales.gov.uk/subisocialpolicysocialser vices/content/workforce/degree-social-work-e.rtf, accessed 29 April 2004.

47 Hites (2001) 'Evaluating environmental chemistry textbooks'.

48 Koeske (1994) 'Some recommendations for improving measurement validation'.

49 Hites (2001) 'Evaluating environmental chemistry textbooks'.

50 Ferrell et al (1999) 'Analysis of end-of-life content in nursing textbooks'; Ferrell et al (2000) 'Current reviews'; Kramer et al (2003) 'Analysis of end-of-life content'.

51 Carron et al (1999) 'End-of-life care'.

52 Wright et al (1997) 'Textbook adoption and other landmark decisions'.

53 Ruffolo et al (1994) 'Scapegoating of mothers'.

54 Wright et al (1997) 'Textbook adoption and other landmark decisions'.

55 John Smith Bookshop, University of Glasgow; John Smith Bookshop, University of Strathclyde, Jordanhill campus; and Waterstones, Sauchiehall Street, Glasgow branch.

56 Dalrymple, J. and Burke, B. (1995) *Anti-oppressive practice: Social care and the law,* Buckingham: Open University Press.

57 Davies, M. (ed) (2000) *The Blackwell encyclopaedia of social work,* Oxford: Blackwell Publishers.

58 Jackson, S. (2000) 'Assessment in childcare', in M. Davies (ed) *Blackwell encyclopaedia.*

59 Griggs, L. (2000) 'Assessment in community care', in M. Davies (ed) *Blackwell encyclopaedia.*

60 Kemshall, H. and Knight, C. (2000) 'Assessment in work with offenders', in M. Davies (ed) *Blackwell encyclopaedia.*

61 Parton, N. and O'Byrne, P. (2000) *Constructive social work: Towards a new practice,* Basingstoke: Macmillan.

62 Adams, R., Dominelli, L. and Payne, M. (2001) *Critical practice in social work*, Basingstoke: Palgrave.

63 Milner, J. and O'Byrne, P. (2001) 'Assessment and planning', in R. Adams, L. Dominelli and M. Payne (eds) *Critical practice in social work*, Basingstoke: Palgrave.

64 O'Sullivan, T. (2001) 'Managing risk and decision making', in R. Adams, L. Dominelli and M. Payne (eds) *Critical practice in social work*, Basingstoke: Palgrave.

65 Hepworth, D.H., Rooney, R.H. and Larsen, J.A. (2002) *Direct social work practice: Theory and skills* (6th edn), Pacific Grove, CA: Brooks/Cole Publishing.

66 Fook, J. (2002) *Social work: Critical theory and practice*, London: Sage Publications.

67 Coulshed, V. and Orme, J. (1998) *Social work practice: An introduction* (3rd edn), Basingstoke: Macmillan.

68 Parker and Bradley (2003) *Social work practice.*

69 Compton, B.R. and Galaway, B. (1999) *Social work processes* (6th edn), London: Brooks/Cole Publishing.

70 Trevithick. P. (2000) *Social work skills: A practice handbook*, Buckingham: Open University Press.

71 Middleton, L. (1997) *The art of assessment*, Birmingham: Venture Press.

72 Milner and O'Byrne (2002) *Assessment in social work.*

73 Kemshall, H. and Pritchard, J. (eds) (1996) *Good practice in risk assessment and management 1,* London: Jessica Kingsley Publishers.

74 Kemshall, H. and Pritchard, J. (eds) (1997) *Good practice in risk assessment and management 2: Protection, rights and responsibilities,* London: Jessica Kingsley Publishers.

75 Clifford, D. (1998) *Social assessment theory and practice: A multi-disciplinary framework*, Aldershot: Ashgate Publishing Limited.

76 Smale, G., Tuson, G. and Statham, D. (2000) *Social work and social problems: Working towards social inclusion and social change*, Basingstoke: Macmillan.

77 Parsloe, P. (ed) (1999) *Risk assessment in social care and social work*, London: Jessice Kingsley Publishers.

78 Ferrell, B., Virani, R., Grant, M. and Juarez, G. (2000) 'Current reviews: analysis of palliative care content in nursing textbooks', *Journal of Palliative Care*, vol 16, pp 39-47.

[79] Kramer et al (2003) 'Analysis of end-of-life content'.
[80] Milner and O'Byrne (2002) *Assessment in social work*, p 8.
[81] Davies (2000) *Blackwell encyclopaedia*.
[82] Compton and Galaway (1999) *Social work processes*.
[83] Parker and Bradley (2003) *Social work practice*.
[84] Middleton (1997) *Art of assessment*.
[85] Hepworth et al (2002) *Direct social work practice*.
[86] Milner and O'Byrne (2002) *Assessment in social work*.
[87] Clifford (1998) *Social assessment*; Fook (2002) *Social work*; Kemshall and Pritchard (1996) *Good practice 1*; Kemshall and Pritchard (1997) *Good practice 2*.
[88] Clifford (1998) *Social assessment*.
[89] Compton and Galaway (1999) *Social work processes*.
[90] Hepworth et al (2002) *Direct social work practice*.
[91] American Psychiatric Association (1994) *Diagnostic and statistical manual of mental disorders: DSM-IV*, Washington, DC: American Psychiatric Association.
[92] Fook (2002) *Social work*.
[93] Milner and O'Byrne (2002) *Assessment in social work*, p 6.
[94] Coulshed and Orme (1998) *Social work practice*, p 21.
[95] Kemshall and Knight (2000) 'Assessment'.
[96] Griggs (2000) 'Assessment'.
[97] Middleton (1997) *Art of assessment*.
[98] Clifford (1998) *Social assessment*; Smale et al (2000) *Social work and social problems*.
[99] Smale et al (2000) *Social work and social problems*, p 132.
[100] Compton and Galaway (1999) *Social work processes*, p 253.
[101] Hepworth et al (2002) *Direct social work practice*, p 188.
[102] Smale et al (2000) *Social work and social problems*, p 109.
[103] Kemshall and Knight (2000) 'Assessment', p 23.
[104] O'Sullivan (2001) 'Managing risk', p 272.
[105] Fook (2002) *Social work*, p 118.
[106] Parton and O'Byrne (2000) *Constructive social work*.
[107] Coulshed and Orme (1998) *Social work practice*; Dalrymple and Burke (1995) *Anti-oppressive practice*.
[108] Milner and O'Byrne (2001) 'Assessment and planning'; O'Sullivan (2001) 'Managing risk'.
[109] Milner and O'Byrne (2002) *Assessment in social work*.

[110] Coulshed and Orme (1998) *Social work practice*; Parton and O'Byrne (2000) *Constructive social work*; Smale et al (2000) *Social work and social problems*.

[111] Milner and O'Byrne (2001) 'Assessment and planning'; Milner and O'Byrne (2002) *Assessment in social work*.

[112] Fook (2002) *Social work*.

[113] Milner and O'Byrne (2002) *Assessment in social work*.

[114] Milner and O'Byrne (2001) 'Assessment and planning'; Milner and O'Byrne (2002) *Assessment in social work*.

[115] Parker and Bradley (2003) *Social work practice*.

[116] Compton and Galaway (1999) *Social work processes*; Hepworth et al (2002) *Direct social work practice*.

[117] Milner and O'Byrne (2002) *Assessment in social work*.

[118] Hepworth et al (2002) *Direct social work practice*.

[119] Griggs (2000) 'Assessment'; Jackson (2000) 'Assessment'; Kemshall and Knight (2000) 'Assessment'; Middleton (1997) *Art of assessment*.

[120] Compton and Galaway (1999) *Social work processes*; Hepworth et al (2002) *Direct social work practice*; Parker and Bradley (2003) *Social work practice*.

[121] Jackson (2000) 'Assessment'; Kemshall and Pritchard (1996) *Good practice 1*; Kemshall and Pritchard (1997) *Good practice 2*; Parker and Bradley (2003) *Social work practice*.

[122] O'Sullivan (2001) 'Managing risk'.

[123] Coulshed and Orme (1998) *Social work practice*.

[124] Middleton (1997) *Art of assessment*.

[125] Fook (2002) *Social work*.

[126] Clifford (1998) *Social assessment*.

[127] Kemshall and Knight (2000) 'Assessment', p 23.

[128] Middleton (1997) *Art of assessment*.

[129] Griggs (2000) 'Assessment'; Hepworth et al (2002) *Direct social work practice*; Milner and O'Byrne (2001) 'Assessment and planning'; Parton and O'Byrne (2000) *Constructive social work*.

[130] Kemshall and Pritchard (1996) *Good practice 1*; Kemshall and Pritchard (1997) *Good practice 2*.

[131] Adams et al (2001) *Critical practice*; Clifford (1998) *Social assessment*.

[132] Parton and O'Byrne (2000) *Constructive social work.*

[133] Kemshall and Knight (2000) 'Assessment'.

[134] Hepworth et al (2002) *Direct social work practice.*

[135] Compton and Galaway (1999) *Social work processes*; Coulshed and Orme (1998) *Social work practice*; Fook (2002) *Social work*; Middleton (1997) *Art of assessment.*

[136] Smale et al (2000) *Social work and social problems.*

[137] Trevithick (2000) *Social work skills.*

[138] Dalrymple and Burke (1995) *Anti-oppressive practice*; Parker and Bradley (2003) *Social work practice.*

[139] Kemshall and Pritchard (1996) *Good practice 1*; Kemshall and Pritchard (1997) *Good practice 2*; Parker and Bradley (2003) *Social work practice*; Trevithick (2000) *Social work skills.*

[140] Hepworth et al (2002) Direct *social work practice*; Smale et al (2000) *Social work and social problems.*

[141] Middleton (1997) *Art of assessment*; Milner and O'Byrne (2002) *Assessment in social work.*

[142] Clifford (1998) *Social assessment*; Coulshed and Orme (1998) *Social work practice.*

[143] Adams et al (2001) *Critical practice in social work*; Dalrymple and Burke (1995) *Anti-oppressive practice*; Davies (2000) *Blackwell enyclopaedia.*

[144] Fook (2002) *Social work*; Parton and O'Byrne (2000) *Constructive social work.*

[145] Milner and O'Byrne (2001) 'Assessment and planning'; O'Sullivan (2001) 'Managing risk'; Parton and O'Byrne (2000) *Constructive social work*; Smale et al (2000) *Social work and social problems.*

[146] Coulshed and Orme (1998) *Social work practice*; Jackson (2000) 'Assessment'.

[147] Clifford (1998) *Social assessment.*

[148] Trevithick (2000) *Social work skills.*

[149] Dalrymple and Burke (1995) *Anti-oppressive practice*; Kemshall and Pritchard (1996) *Good practice 1*; Kemshall and Pritchard (1997) *Good practice 2*; Milner and O'Byrne (2002) *Assessment in social work.*

[150] Milner and O'Byrne (2002) *Assessment in social work*, p 23.

[151] Fook (2002) *Social work.*

[152] Dalrymple and Burke (1995) *Anti-oppressive practice*, p 120.

153 Jackson (2000) 'Assessment', p 20.

154 Hepworth et al (2002) *Direct social work practice.*

155 Compton and Galaway (1999) *Social work processes.*

156 Dalrymple and Burke (1995) *Anti-oppressive practice*; Parker and Bradley (2003) *Social work practice.*

157 Dalrymple and Burke (1995) *Anti-oppressive practice*; Middleton (1997) *Art of assessment.*

158 Parker and Bradley (2003) *Social work practice.*

159 Department of Health (2002) *Requirements for social work training.*

160 Scottish Executive (2003) *The framework for social work education in Scotland.*

161 Department of Health, Social Services and Public Safety (2003) *Northern Ireland framework specification for the Degree in Social Work.*

162 National Assembly for Wales (2003) *Requirements for an award of a Degree in Social Work.*

163 Milner and O'Byrne (2002) *Assessment in social work.*

164 Clifford (1998) *Social assessment*; Coulshed and Orme (1998) *Social work practice*; Jackson (2000) 'Assessment'; Kemshall and Pritchard (1996) *Good practice 1*; Parton and O'Byrne (2000) *Constructive social work*; Smale et al (2000) *Social work and social problems.*

165 Coulshed and Orme (1998) *Social work practice.*

166 Kemshall and Knight (2000) 'Assessment'.

167 Trevithick (2000) *Social work skills.*

168 Hepworth et al (2002) *Direct social work practice*; Milner and O'Byrne (2001) 'Assessment and planning'; O'Sullivan (2001) 'Managing risk'.

169 Compton and Galaway (1999) *Social work processes*; Fook (2002) *Social work.*

170 Milner and O'Byrne (2002) *Assessment in social work.*

171 Dalrymple and Burke (1995) *Anti-oppressive practice*; Kemshall and Knight (2000) 'Assessment'; Middleton (1997) *Art of assessment.*

172 Compton and Galaway (1999) *Social work processes*; Fook (2002) *Social work*; Hepworth et al (2002) *Direct social work practice.*

[173] Kemshall and Pritchard (1996) *Good practice 1*; Kemshall and Pritchard (1997) *Good practice 2*; Milner and O'Byrne (2001) 'Assessment and planning'; O'Sullivan (2001) 'Managing risk'; Parton and O'Byrne (2000) *Constructive social work*; Parker and Bradley (2003) *Social work practice*; Smale et al (2000) *Social work and social problems*.

[174] Clifford (1998) *Social assessment*, p xx.

[175] Parker and Bradley (2003) *Social work practice*.

[176] A genogram is a map of an intergenerational family system, see Hartman, A. and Laird, J. (1983) *Family-centered social work practice*, New York, NY: The Free Press.

[177] An ecomap is a map of the systems which interact with an individual or family, see Hartman and Laird (1983) *Family-centered social work practice*.

[178] Hepworth et al (2002) *Direct social work practice*; Parker and Bradley (2003) *Social work practice*.

[179] Parker and Bradley (2003) *Social work practice*, p 51.

[180] Hepworth et al (2002) *Direct social work practice*.

[181] Coulshed and Orme (1998) *Social work practice*.

[182] Parker and Bradley (2003) *Social work practice*, p 22.

[183] Milner and O'Byrne (2002) *Assessment in social work*.

[184] Clifford (1998) *Social assessment*.

[185] Compton and Galaway (1999) *Social work processes*.

[186] Hepworth et al (2002) *Direct social work practice*.

[187] Parker and Bradley (2003) *Social work practice*.

[188] O'Sullivan (2001) 'Managing risk'.

[189] Jackson (2000) 'Assessment'.

[190] Kemshall and Knight (2000) 'Assessment'.

[191] Kemshall and Pritchard (1996) *Good practice 1*; Kemshall and Pritchard (1997) *Good practice 2*; Smale et al (2000) *Social work and social problems*.

[192] Middleton (1997) *Art of assessment*.

[193] Fook (2002) *Social work*; Parton and O'Byrne (2000) *Constructive social work*.

[194] Dalrymple and Burke (1995) *Anti-oppressive practice*; Griggs (2000) 'Assessment'.

[195] DeNeve, K. and Heppner, M.J. (1997) 'Role play simulations: the assessment of an active learning technique and comparisons with traditional lectures', *Innovative Higher Education*, vol 21, pp 231-46; Lord, T.R. (1998) 'How to build a better mousetrap: changing the way science is taught through constructivism', *Contemporary Education*, vol 69, pp 134-6.

[196] Fook (2002) *Social work*; Kemshall and Pritchard (1996) *Good practice 1*; Kemshall and Pritchard (1997) *Good practice 2*; Parker and Bradley (2003) *Social work practice*.

[197] Clifford (1998) *Social assessment*; Compton and Galaway (1999) *Social work processes*; Dalrymple and Burke (1995) *Anti-oppressive practice*.

[198] Kemshall and Pritchard (1997) *Good practice 2*.

[199] Milner and O'Byrne (2001) 'Assessment and planning'; O'Sullivan (2001) 'Managing risk'.

[200] Clifford (1998) *Social assessment*.

[201] Compton and Galaway (1999) *Social work processes*; Coulshed and Orme (1998) *Social work practice*; Fook (2002) *Social work*; Hepworth et al (2002) *Direct social work practice*; Kemshall and Pritchard (1996) *Good practice 1*; Kemshall and Pritchard (1997) *Good practice 2*; Milner and O'Byrne (2002) *Assessment in social work*; Parker and Bradley (2003) *Social work practice*.

[202] Compton and Galaway (1999) *Social work processes*; Coulshed and Orme (1998) *Social work practice*.

[203] Kemshall and Pritchard (1996) *Good practice 1*.

[204] Hepworth et al (2002) *Direct social work practice*.

[205] Dalrymple and Burke (1995) *Anti-oppressive practice*.

[206] Hepworth et al (2002) *Direct social work practice*.

[207] Parton and O'Byrne (2000) *Constructive social work*.

[208] Trevithick (2000) *Social work skills*.

[209] For example, Beresford, P. and Croft, S. (1993) *Citizen involvement: A practical guide for change*, Basingstoke: Macmillan.

[210] Dalrymple and Burke (1995) *Anti-oppressive practice*.

[211] Middleton (1997) *Art of assessment*; Parker and Bradley (2003) *Social work practice*.

[212] Coulshed and Orme (1998) *Social work practice*; Dalrymple and Burke (1995) *Anti-oppressive practice*.

[213] Dalrymple and Burke (1995) *Anti-oppressive practice.*

[214] Adams et al (2001) *Critical practice*; Davies (2000) *Blackwell encylopaedia*; Hepworth et al (2002) *Direct social work practice.*

[215] Clifford (1998) *Social assessment*; Compton and Galaway (1999) *Social work processes*; Fook (2002) *Social work*; Kemshall and Pritchard (1996) *Good practice 1*; Kemshall and Pritchard (1997) *Good practice 2*; Smale et al (2000) *Social work and social problems.*

[216] Trevithick (2000) *Social work skills.*

[217] Milner and O'Byrne (2002) *Assessment in social work.*

[218] Department of Health et al (2000) *Framework for the assessment of children in need and their families.*

[219] Trevithick (2000) *Social work skills.*

[220] Parker and Bradley (2003) *Social work practice.*

[221] Coulshed and Orme (1998) *Social work practice.*

[222] Compton and Galaway (1999) *Social work processes*; Hepworth et al (2002) *Direct social work practice.*

[223] Wachholz and Mullaly (2000) 'The politics of the textbook'.

[224] Walker, S. and Beckett, C. (2004) *Social work assessment and intervention,* Lyme Regis: Russell House Publishers.

[225] Smale, G., Tuson, G., Biehal, N. and Marsh, P. (1993) *Empowerment, assessment, care management and the skilled worker,* London: HMSO.

[226] Smale et al (2000) *Social work and social problems.*

[227] Taylor, B.J. and Devine, T. (1993) *Assessing needs and planning care in social work,* Aldershot: Arena.

[228] Payne, M. (1997) *Modern social work theory* (2nd edn), London: Macmillan.

[229] Stepney, P. and Ford, D. (2000) *Social work models, methods and theories,* Lyme Regis: Russell House Publishing

[230] Davies, M. (ed) (2002) *The Blackwell companion to social work* (2nd edn), Oxford: Blackwell Publishers.

[231] Beresford, P. and Trevillion, S. (1995) *Developing skills for community care,* Aldershot: Arena; Payne, M. (2000) *Teamwork in multiprofessional care,* Basingstoke: Palgrave.

[232] For example, eight recruiting companies offering social work employment in the UK advertised in the June 2004 edition of *Australian Social Work*. Similar numbers of advertisements have been appearing in each edition for a number of years and Australia is only one of a number of countries from where social workers are being sought.

[233] Department of Health et al (2000) *Framework for the assessment of children in need and their families.*

[234] The 1989 edition of Compton and Galaway's *Social work processes* is referred to in the *Framework for the assessment of children in need and their families*. Assessment is similarly defined in both the 1989 and 1999 editions of *Social work processes.*

[235] Levin, E. (2004) *Resource guide 2: Involving service users and carers in social work education*, London: Social Care Institute for Excellence.

[236] Croft, S. and Beresford, P. (2002) 'Service users' perspectives', in M. Davies (ed) (2002) *The Blackwell companion to social work* (2nd edn), Oxford: Blackwell Publishers; Richards, S. (2000) 'Bridging the divide: elders and the assessment process', *British Journal of Social Work*, vol 30, pp 37-49; Stanley, N. (1999) 'User-practitioner transactions in the new culture of community care', *British Journal of Social Work*, vol 29, pp 417-35.

[237] Benbenishty, R., Osmo, R. and Gold, N. (2003) 'Rationales provided for risk assessments and for recommended interventions in child protection: a comparison between Canadian and Israeli professionals', *British Journal of Social Work*, vol 33, pp 137-55.

[238] Sheldon, B. and Chilvers, R. (2000) *Evidence-based social care: A study of prospects and problems*, Lyme Regis, Dorset: Russell House Publishing.

[239] Rosen, A. (1994) 'Knowledge use in direct practice', *Social Service Review*, vol 68, pp 561-77; Rosen, A., Proctor, E.E., Morrow-Howell, N. and Staudt, M. (1995) 'Rationales for practice decisions: variations in knowledge use by decision task and social work service', *Research on Social Work Practice*, vol 5, pp 501-23.

[240] Benbenishty et al (2003) 'Rationales provided for risk assessments'.

[241] Walter, I., Nutley, S., Percy-Smith, J., McNeish, D. and Frost, S. (2004) *Knowledge review 3: Research utilisation and the social care workforce*, London: Social Care Institute for Excellence.

242 Berg, M., Horstman, K., Plass, S. and Heusden, M.V. (2000) 'Guidelines, professionals and the production of objectivity: standardisation and the professionalisation of insurance medicine', *Sociology of Health and Illness*, vol 22, pp 765-91.

243 Lyons, P., Doueck, H.J., Koster, A.J., Witzky, M.K. and Kelly, P.L. (1999) 'The child well-being scales as a clinical tool and a management information system', *Child Welfare*, vol 78, pp 241-58.

244 Berg et al (2000) 'Guidelines'.

245 Gimpel, J. (1997) 'The Risk Assessment and Cost Benefit Act of 1995: regulatory, reform and the legislation of science', *Journal of Legislation*, vol 23, pp 61-91.

246 Campbell, S.M., Roland, M.O. and Buetow, S.A. (2000) 'Defining quality of care' *Social Science and Medicine*, vol 51, pp 1611-25.

247 Buckley, H. (2000) 'Child protection: an unreflective practice', *Social Work Education*, vol 19, pp 253-63.

248 Parry-Jones, B. and Soulsby, J. (2001) 'Needs-led assessment: the challenges and the reality', *Health and Social Care in the Community*, vol 9, pp 414-28.

249 Gumpert, C.H. and Lindblad, F. (2001) 'Communication between courts and expert witnesses in legal proceedings concerning child sexual abuse in Sweden: a case review', *Child Abuse and Neglect*, vol 25, pp 1497-516.

250 Velasquez, J.S. and Velasquez, C.P. (1980) 'Application of a bicultural assessment framework to social work practice with Hispanics', *Family Relations*, vol 29, pp 598-603; Wilkinson, I. (2000) 'The Darlington Family Assessment System: clinical guidelines for practitioners', *Journal of Family Therapy*, vol 22, pp 211-24.

251 Wilkinson (2000) 'Darlington Family Assessment System', p 223.

252 Berg et al (2000) 'Guidelines'.

253 Macdonald, G. (2001) *Effective interventions for child abuse and neglect: An evidence-based approach to planning and evaluating interventions*, Chichester: John Wiley and Sons.

254 Jörg, F., Boeije, H.R., Huijsman, R., de Weert, G.H. and Schrijvers, A.J.P. (2002) 'Objectivity in needs assessment practice: admission to a residential home', *Health and Social Care in the Community*, vol 10, pp 445-56.

[255] Seddon, D. and Robinson, C.A. (2001) 'Carers of older people with dementia: assessment and the *Carers Act*', *Health and Social Care in the Community*, vol 9, pp 151-8.

[256] Munro, E. (1998) 'Improving social worker's knowledge base in child protection work', *British Journal of Social Work*, vol 28, pp 89-105, here p 101.

[257] Clifford (1998) *Social assessment*, p 5.

[258] Berg, M. (1997) 'Problems and promises of the protocol', *Social Science and Medicine*, vol 44, pp 1081-88; Berg et al (2000) 'Guidelines'.

[259] Scannapieco, M. and Hegar, R.L. (1996) 'A nontraditional assessment framework for formal kinship homes', *Child Welfare*, vol 75, pp 567-82; Witter, S. (2004) 'Developing a framework for monitoring child poverty: results from a study in Uganda', *Children and Society*, vol 18, pp 3-15.

[260] Mailick, M.D. (1988) 'Assessment: a critical component of clinical social work practice with physically ill adolescents', *Child and Adolescent Social Work*, vol 5, pp 229-39.

[261] Maher, C.A. and Illback, R.J. (1981) 'Planning for the delivery of special services in public schools', *Evaluation and Program Planning*, vol 4, pp 249-59.

[262] Horwath, J. and Morrison, T. (2000) 'Identifying and implementing pathways for organizational change: using the *Framework for the assessment of children in need and their families* as a case example', *Child and Family Social Work*, vol 5, pp 245-54.

[263] Nicholas, E. (2003) 'An outcome focus in carer assessment and review: value and challenge', *British Journal of Social Work*, vol 33, pp 31-47.

[264] Macdonald (2001) *Effective Interventions*, pp 238-9.

[265] Nicholas (2003) 'An outcome focus'.

[266] Skinner, H., Steinhauer, P. and Sitarenios, G. (2000) 'Family assessment measure (FAM) and process model of family functioning', *Journal of Family Therapy*, vol 22, pp 190-210, here p 196.

[267] Wilkinson (2000) 'Darlington Family Assessment System', p 215.

[268] Department of Health et al (2000) *Framework for the assessment of children in need and their families*.

[269] Department of Health (2001) *A practitioner's guide to carers' assessments under the Carers and Disabled Children Act 2000*, London: Department of Health.

[270] Effective Interventions Unit (2002) *Integrated care for drug users: Integration principles and practice*, Edinburgh: Effective Interventions Unit, Substance Misuse Division, Scottish Executive.

[271] Department of Health (2001) *National service framework for older people*, London: Department of Health.

[272] Department of Health (2001) *A practitioner's guide to carers' assessments*, p 1.

[273] Department of Health et al (2000) *Framework for the assessment of children in need and their families*, p 26.

[274] Department of Health et al (2000) *Framework for the assessment of children in need and their families*, p ix.

[275] Department of Health et al (2000) *Framework for the assessment of children in need and their families*, p 29.

[276] Effective Interventions Unit (2002) *Integrated care for drug users*, p 73.

[277] Department of Health (2001) *A practitioner's guide to carers' assessments*, p 9.

[278] Department of Health et al (2000) *Framework for the assessment of children in need and their families*, p 16.

[279] Department of Health (2000) *Framework for the assessment of children in need and their families: Guidance notes and glossary for referral and information record, initial assessment record and core assessment record*, London: The Stationery Office; Department of Health and Cleaver, H. (2000) *Assessment recording forms*, London: The Stationery Office; Department of Health, Cox, A. and Bentovim, A. (2000) *The family assessment pack of questionnaires and scales*, London: The Stationery Office.

[280] Effective Interventions Unit (2003) *Integrated care for drug users: Assessment. Digest of tools used in the assessment process and core data sets*, Edinburgh: Effective Interventions Unit, Substance Misuse Division, Scottish Executive.

[281] Department of Health (2001) *A practitioner's guide to carers' assessments*, p 11.

[282] Department of Health et al (2000) *Framework for the assessment of children in need and their families*, p 53.

[283] Department of Health (2001) *National service framework for older people*, p 1.

[284] Department of Health et al (2000) *Framework for the assessment of children in need and their families*, p viii.

[285] Department of Health (2001) *A practitioner's guide to carers' assessments*, p 7.

[286] Department of Health et al (2000) *Framework for the assessment of children in need and their families*, p 34.

[287] Department of Health (2001) *A practitioner's guide to carers' assessments*, p 11.

[288] Department of Health (2001) *National service framework for older people*, p 11.

[289] Department of Health et al (2000) *Framework for the assessment of children in need and their families*, p 16.

[290] Fook, J., Ryan, M. and Hawkins, L. (1997) 'Towards a theory of social work expertise' *British Journal of Social Work*, vol 27, pp 399-417.

[291] Katz, I. (1997) *Current issues in comprehensive assessment*, London: NSPCC.

[292] Horwath, J. (2002) 'Maintaining a focus on the child?', *Child Abuse Review*, vol 11, pp 195-213, here pp 203-4.

[293] Gordon, R. and Hendry, E. (2001) 'Supervising assessments of children and families: the role of the front line manager', in J. Horwarth (ed) *The child's world: Assessing children in need*, London: Jessica Kingsley Publishers.

[294] Horwath (2002) 'Maintaining a focus'.

[295] Howe, D. (1992) 'Child abuse and the bureaucratisation of social work', *Sociological Review*, vol 40, pp 490-508, here pp 506-7.

[296] Garrett, P.M. (2003) 'Swimming with dolphins: the assessment framework, New Labour and new tools for social work with children and families', *British Journal of Social Work*, vol 33, pp 441-63; Rose, W. (2002) 'Two steps forward, one step back: issues for policy and practice', in H. Ward and W. Rose (eds) *Approaches to needs assessment in children's services*, London: Jessica Kingsley Publishers.

[297] Qureshi, H. (2004) 'Evidence in policy and practice: what kinds of research designs?', *Journal of Social Work*, vol 4, pp 7-23.

[298] Buckley (2000) 'Child protection'.

[299] Abrahams, R., Capitman, J., Leutz, W. and Macko, P. (1989) 'Variations in care planning practice in the social/HMO: an explanatory study', *Gerontologist*, vol 29, pp 725-36.

[300] Horwath (2002) 'Maintaining a focus'.

[301] Horwath and Morrison (2000) 'Identifying and implementing pathways'.

[302] Morrison, T. (2000) 'Working together to safeguard children: challenges and changes for inter-agency co-ordination in child protection', *Journal of Interprofessional Care*, vol 14, pp 363-73.

[303] See Appendix 4 for details of accompanying documents for each framework.

[304] Horwath (2002) 'Maintaining a focus'.

[305] Compton and Galaway (1999) *Social work processes*; Hepworth et al (2002) *Direct social work practice.*

[306] Chakrabarti, M. (ed) (2001) *Social welfare: Scottish perspectives*, Aldershot: Ashgate; Ford, P. and Hayes, P. (1996) *Educating for social work: Arguments for optimism*, Aldershot: Avebury; Stepney and Ford (2000) *Social work models.*

Appendix 1:
Textbooks including chapters or distinct sections on assessment

Textbook
Critical practice in social work (2001) Basingstoke: Palgrave.[62]

Editors
Robert Adams, Lena Dominelli and Malcolm Payne.

Editors' affiliations at time of publication
Robert Adams is Professor of Human Services Development at the University of Lincoln and Visiting Professor of Social Work at the University of Teesside, England.

Lena Dominelli is Professor of Social and Community Development and Director of the Centre for International Social and Community Development, Department of Social Work Studies at the University of Southampton, England.

Malcolm Payne is Professor of Applied Community Studies and Head of the Department of Applied Community Studies at Manchester Metropolitan University, England.

Edition
First edition.

Cost
£18.99.

Intended audience
According to the back cover, "with its extensive scope and powerful practice focus, this is an indispensable companion for students and practitioners alike".

Number of pages – total
358 including Bibliography, Author Index and Subject Index (pp 312-58) plus Contents, Notes on Contributors and Introduction (pp v-xxii).

Number of pages – assessment
There are two chapters focusing on assessment which have a combined total of 17 pages:

Chapter 26: Assessment and planning, by Judith Milner and Patrick O'Byrne, pp 261-8.[63]

Chapter 27: Managing risk and decision making, by Terence O'Sullivan, pp 269-77.[64]

Authors' affiliations at time of publication
Judith Milner is a former senior lecturer in social work at the University of Huddersfield, England, now working as a counsellor and freelance trainer.

Patrick O'Byrne is a former senior lecturer in social work at the University of Huddersfield, England, now working as a family mediator.

Terence O'Sullivan is senior lecturer in social work at the University of Lincoln, England.

Key headings within chapters on assessment
Chapter 26: Assessment and planning
- Introduction
- Case example
- What the work involves
- Concepts to be questioned
- Social construction and assessment
- Case example revisited
- Implications for workers or managers
- Resources
- Values
- Morale
- Certainty

- Listening
- Safety
- Language
- The future
- Causes and explanations
- Greater responsibility
- Conclusion
- Further reading.

Chapter 27: Managing risk and decision making
- Introduction
- Case example
- What is meant by risk?
- What are the social contexts of the decision making?
- How are risks to be assessed?
- The use of risk assessment instruments
- How is risk to be analysed?
- What use to make of research findings?
- What approach to risk management is to be taken?
- Conclusion
- Further reading.

Definitions of assessment

The following definitions are provided:

O'Sullivan proposed that:

> Assessment is a basis for decision making and different types of assessment can be distinguished by their purpose.... The result of any assessment is a particular representation of reality... (O'Sullivan, 2001, p 272)

Rather than provide a definition, Milner and O'Byrne note the current fluidity around how assessment is defined:

> There is probably no area of social work where debate rages so fiercely as in assessment. Agencies have been attempting to structure assessments, providing checklists and guidelines. Meanwhile government

has redefined assessment with each new piece of legislation, sometimes stressing need, sometimes eligibility. The professional task itself
is riddled with dilemmas and tensions. If a worker is too idealistic,
recommendations, although laudable, will be too costly. Workers are
trained to be needs led, but agencies seem to be risk and resource led.
(Milner and O'Byrne, 2001, p 261)

Timing of assessment

Milner and O'Byrne note that assessment should be an ongoing process
but constraints often result in it being a one-off process. Conversely, risk
assessments bring together information that assesses the risks involved
in various options at a particular point in time, recognising that these
assessments may need to be revised in the future.

Theoretical underpinnings

Milner and O'Byrne propose a constructionist approach to assessment,
which draws on solution-based and narrative approaches to social work.
O'Sullivan also sees the need to go beyond tick-box approaches to assessment, arguing that both strengths and risks need to be identified in
a risk assessment, along with an understanding of the social context in
which assessment decisions are being made.

Information obtained during the assessment process

Milner and O'Byrne critique what they consider to be prevailing practice,
which involves focus on problems and places little emphasis on strengths.
They also call for more of a focus on the future rather than focusing on
the past, whereas O'Sullivan calls for a critical rather than a mechanistic
use of checklists that have been developed to assess risk.

Risk assessment

There is an entire chapter devoted to the topic of risk assessment.

Multidisciplinary assessment

A chapter on multidisciplinary working immediately precedes the
chapters on assessment.

Involvement of users and carers in the process
In both chapters, working in partnership with users and carers is considered critical.

User and carer perspectives of the assessment process
Not discussed.

Evidence bases
Both chapters draw on current writings and use a case-study approach to demonstrate the effectiveness of the proposed approaches. O'Sullivan includes a useful section on how research findings can be used in risk assessment.

Inclusion of case studies
Each chapter is structured around a case study.

Anti-discriminatory/anti-oppressive practice
The approach to assessment in both chapters is consistent with anti-discriminatory/anti-oppressive practice, although there is no explicit discussion of such.

Languages other than English and use of interpreters
Not mentioned.

Legislation/legal frameworks
Legislative frameworks are mentioned but not specific legislation.

Accuracy
Both chapters address current debates on assessment in the UK.

Comprehensiveness
Both chapters introduce the readers to some current practice debates within the UK. Readers wanting further information on the assessment process would need to look elsewhere, but recommended further reading is provided.

Durability

The material in both chapters is unlikely to date rapidly, although the reader might anticipate some changes in emphasis if a subsequent edition was to be produced in a few years.

Transferability

Although written within the UK policy and practice context, these chapters on assessment would be readily accessible to social work students and practitioners elsewhere.

Recommended further reading

Each chapter provides a short list of additional readings for readers wanting further information about assessment.

Learning exercises

Not provided.

Outstanding features

Focusing each chapter around a case study enables an explicit demonstration of the integration of theory and practice.

Shortcomings

Both chapters assume a basic level of knowledge about the assessment process.

Textbook

Social work processes (1999) London: Brooks/Cole Publishing.[69]

Authors

Beulah R. Compton and Burt Galaway.

Authors' affiliations at time of publication

Beulah R. Compton is from the University of Mississipi, USA.

Burt Galaway is from the University of Manitoba, Canada.

Edition
Sixth edition.

Cost
£36.00.

Intended audience
Social work students and educators.

Number of pages – total
560 including Appendices and Index (pp 509-60) plus Contents, Exhibits, Contributors and Preface (pp vii-xxviii).

Number of pages – assessment
There are 48 pages in Chapter 10: Data collection and assessment, pp 253-300.

Key headings within chapter on assessment
- Chapter preview
- Assessment
- Definition
- Data and information
- The purpose of assessment
- Assessment and diagnosis
- Assessment as a continuous process
- Types of assessment
- Types of data
- Client wants and desired solutions
- Exploring the presenting problem
- Discovering the strengths
- Data collection
- Locating the data
- Interviewing in social work
- Other data collection tools
- Data collection by applicants
- Process data and decision making
- Role of the applicant
- Use of knowledge

- Assessment instruments
- Assessment as negotiation
- Assessment as a continuous process
- Partialization
- Sequencing of service plans
- Chapter summary
- A look forward
- Reading 10.1: Family group decision making
- Reading 10.2: The clinical utility of models and methods of assessment in managed care
- Learning exercises
- References.

Definitions of assessment

The following definition is provided:

> Assessment – the collection and processing of data to provide information for use in making decisions about the nature of the problem and what is to be done about it – is a cognitive, thinking process; it involves thinking about data that have been collected. The outcome of assessment is a service plan, which provides a definition of the problem for work, objectives or solutions to be achieved, and an action plan to accomplish the objectives. (Compton and Galaway, 1999, p 253)

Timing of assessment

Assessment is a continuous process.

Theoretical underpinnings

A number of theories relating to assessment and planning are discussed, including 'Person in Environment', strengths perspective, systems theory, psychosocial assessment, cognitive behavioural assessment and life model assessment.

Information obtained during the assessment process

In addition to noting some of the domains covered in assessments using the theories outlined above, there is a section on assessment tools.

Risk assessment

Risk is mentioned very briefly and not elaborated on.

Multidisciplinary assessment

This is discussed primarily in relation to the North American concept of 'managed care'.

Involvement of users and carers in the process

Service users are 'applicants' from whom information is obtained. Working in partnership with service users and carers is suggested but as an option rather than an imperative.

User and carer perspectives of the assessment process

Readers are encouraged to seek out service-user perspectives on their experience of the assessment process.

Evidence bases

There are some explicit mentions of empirical research to support some of the material that is presented.

Inclusion of case studies

Several brief case studies are included. An extended example of family group decision making in a Canadian project is also provided.

Anti-discriminatory/anti-oppressive practice

Requests for service in which gender or cross-cultural issues emerge are discussed as ethical concerns. There is no explicit discussion of anti-discriminatory/anti-oppressive practice.

Languages other than English and use of interpreters

Clients from non-English speaking backgrounds and the use of interpreters are not discussed in the chapter on assessment. There is some recognition that clients may speak other languages in the home in the chapter 'Communicating across cultures' but there is no suggestion that interpreters may be needed in order to communicate effectively with some clients.

Legislation/legal frameworks
Not discussed.

Accuracy
Recent research is cited and the authors engage with current debates in North American social work. However, some current emphases in UK social work, for example risk assessment, receive little or no mention.

Comprehensiveness
This text provides the reader with a good understanding of the need not just to collect data but to be able to order it into usable information. However, readers wanting to locate assessment within UK policy and practice emphases would need to obtain this information elsewhere.

Durability
As this text discusses generalised concepts rather than addressing particular policies and legislation, it is not likely to date rapidly.

Transferability
This textbook is written for a North American market, where the philosophical underpinnings and emphases differ somewhat from those from within the UK. For example there is discussion as to whether or not social workers should use DSM-IV in assessments and concerns over the term 'diagnosis'.

Recommended further reading
Two readings are provided in an appendix contained within the chapter on assessment. There are no recommendations for further reading beyond this textbook.

Learning exercises
A number of these are included at the end of the chapter on assessment.

Outstanding features
A strength of the chapter on assessment is that it acknowledges diverse approaches to collecting and using data to form social work assessments.

Shortcomings

The notion of client as 'applicant' has an implicit assumption that clients seek services that does not necessarily reflect the strong emphasis of statutory social work in the UK where social work clients are often involuntary and not necessarily wanting social work services.

Textbook

Social work practice: An introduction (1998) Basingstoke: Macmillan.[67]

Authors

Veronica Coulshed and Joan Orme.

Authors' affiliations at time of publication

Prior to her death, Veronica Coulshed was Head of Applied Social Studies at the University of Sunderland, England.

Joan Orme is Reader in Social Work Studies at the University of Southampton, England.

Edition

Third edition.

Cost

£15.99.

Intended audience

This book aims "to help students and practitioners to apply theory to their practice" (p 1).

Number of pages – total

256 including References and Index (pp 235-56) plus Contents, Lists of Tables and Figures, and Acknowledgements (pp vii-xi).

Number of pages – assessment

There are 29 pages in Chapter 2: Care management: assessment and commissioning services, pp 16-44.

Key headings within the chapter on assessment

- Care management
- Stages of care management
- Assessment
- Initial assessment
- Assessment process
- Assessment in other settings
- Assessments and oppression
- Assessment of need
- Arrangements for assessment
- Multidisciplinary assessments
- Commissioning services
- Monitoring and review.

Definitions of assessment

The following definition is provided:

> Assessment is an ongoing process, in which the client participates, the purpose of which is to understand people in relation to their environment; it is a basis for planning what needs to be done to maintain, improve or bring about change in the person, the environment or both. (Coulshed and Orme, 1998, p 21)

Timing of assessment

Assessment is an ongoing process.

Theoretical underpinnings

Two theoretical models of assessment are discussed: Smale et al's (1993) exchange model of assessment and Vickery's (1976) unified assessment.

Information obtained during the assessment process

It is argued that:

> Assessment in community care involves a shift in emphasis from assessment of an individual to assessment of the individual's circumstances. (Coulshed and Orme, 1998, p 22)

It is noted that social work literature includes extensive lists of different types of information that have been proposed as necessary to obtain during assessments, and what denotes a skilled assessor is the ability to collect sufficient relevant information for the specific context.

Risk assessment
There is brief mention of social workers needing to assess risks but no detailed discussion as to what this involves or issues associated with it.

Multidisciplinary assessment
A section of the chapter is devoted to multidisciplinary assessment.

Involvement of users and carers in the process
The importance of including service users (including children) and their carers in the assessment process is reiterated on a number of occasions.

User and carer perspectives of the assessment process
A lengthy quote from a service user about their involvement with a social worker is included.

Evidence bases
Reference is made to relevant research.

Inclusion of case studies
Several case examples, including one lengthy case study, are included in the chapter on assessment. Service users depicted include an 11-year-old boy who has had several different care placements, an adult male on probation, a woman stroke patient in a hospital and a 91-year-old woman who was living on her own and there were concerns because her home seemed neglected.

Anti-discriminatory/anti-oppressive practice
The need to be sensitive to issues of race and gender and to go beyond stereotypes are discussed.

Languages other than English and use of interpreters

Communications with clients from non-English speaking backgrounds and the use of interpreters are discussed elsewhere in this textbook, but not in the chapter on assessment.

Legislation/legal frameworks

The need to be aware of legislative requirements that impact on the assessment process is stressed, and exemplars of how legislation impacts on assessment are provided.

Accuracy

Although there have been some new policy initiatives since this book was published in 1998, the key ideas and issues maintain relevance. The discussion around access to client records is perhaps even more pertinent than when written, given the Data Protection Act that has been promulgated since the publication of the textbook.

Comprehensiveness

This textbook provides the reader with philosophical and theoretical underpinnings of assessment work. Readers would need to look elsewhere for details on the specific assessment tools mentioned, or on what kinds of data to collect in what circumstances.

Durability

Although some legislation is mentioned as exemplars, the focus is more on general concepts than on specific legislation and policies, and hence will not date rapidly unless there are fundamental shifts in philosophies underpinning social work in the UK.

Transferability

Although written particularly for the UK policy and practice context, this textbook does not rely on readers having a detailed understanding of the UK context.

Recommended further reading

There are a number of suggested further readings made at various stages throughout the chapter on assessment.

Learning exercises
Not included.

Outstanding features
This textbook places assessment in its social context, and hence assessment is portrayed as a skill rather than just a data-collection exercise. There is an emphasis on trying to understand the process from the perspective of service users, and there is an explicit recognition that the service delivery system should be trying to meet the needs of clients, rather than assuming assessments will result in a determination as to how clients should change.

Shortcomings
By focusing on assessment generally, the reader is not provided with knowledge about assessment in specific situations and settings.

Textbook
Anti-oppressive practice: Social care and the law (1995) Buckingham: Open University Press.[56]

Authors
Jane Dalrymple and Beverley Burke.

Authors' affiliations at time of publication
Jane Dalrymple is Director of ASC (Advice, Advocacy and Representation Services for Children and Young People), Manchester, England.

Beverley Burke is Senior Lecturer in Social Work at Liverpool John Moores University, England.

Edition
First edition.

Cost
£19.99.

Intended audience

According to the back cover, "This book is designed for practitioners and carers in social welfare services to help them make the links between the law and their work.... It is a book which is accessible to informal carers, students and professional workers".

Number of pages – total

183 including Bibliography and Index (pp 166-83) plus Contents, Lists of Statues and Cases, Foreword, Preface and Notes on Terminology (pp vii-xvii).

Number of pages – assessment

There are 12 pages in Chapter 9: Assessment, pp 114-25.

Key headings within the chapter on assessment

- What is assessment?
- Assessment is not value free
- Children Act: minimal delay
- Mental health: legalized assault?
- A framework of assessment
- The power of assessment in determining change
- Final thoughts
- Activities.

Definitions of assessment

Assessment involves determination of need by professionals, and this may or may not incorporate the views of service users. The authors quote Pitts (1990):

> Ideally, the assessment should be a forum in which hypotheses are devised and theories tested; a place where conflicting ideas are encouraged. (Pitts, 1990, p 54, cited in Dalrymple and Burke, 1995, p 115)

Timing of assessment

While recognising that there may be situations in which an assessment is required in a specified timeframe, it is proposed that assessment should be an ongoing process.

Theoretical underpinnings

Assessment needs to take into account both the principles of anti-oppressive practice and legislative requirements, and it is acknowledged that this may lead to complex dilemmas, which need to be resolved. A six-point framework for assessment is proposed:

1. Assessment should involve those being assessed.
2. Openness and honesty should permeate the process.
3. Assessment should involve the sharing of values and concerns.
4. There should be acknowledgement of the structural context of the process.
5. The process should be about questioning the basis of the reasons for proposed action, and all those involved should consider alternative courses of action.
6. Assessment should incorporate the different perspectives of the people involved. (Dalrymple and Burke, 1995, p 120)

Information obtained during the assessment process

Apart from noting the need to ascertain the views of service users and carers, there are no specific suggestions as to what information should be collected during the assessment process.

Risk assessment

Although not discussed in the chapter on assessment, it is discussed elsewhere in this textbook.

Multidisciplinary assessment

This is briefly mentioned but not elaborated on.

Involvement of users and carers in the process

The importance of ascertaining the views of service users and carers is stressed, although it is acknowledged that legislative requirements may result in assessments that are more a reflection of the worker's professional judgement than the expressed preferences of service users and their clients.

User and carer perspectives of the assessment process

The chapter on assessment begins with a quote, presumably from a service user, but this is not integrated into the text. A court case in which a service user appealed against the result of an assessment is discussed at one point. Also, in one of the activities, readers who have ever been subject to an assessment are asked to reflect on the process.

Evidence bases

While the authors draw somewhat on academic literature, much of their evidence bases are legal cases and legislation.

Inclusion of case studies

A number of case examples are provided, including cases that have gone to court and are thus in the public arena.

Anti-discriminatory/anti-oppressive practice

This is a key tenet of the chapter on assessment.

Languages other than English and use of interpreters

Not mentioned.

Legislation/legal frameworks

There are explicit references to English legislation.

Accuracy

This textbook was first published in 1995 and the legislation, court cases and policy context cited refer back to the late 1980s and early 1990s. Although there have been some new policy initiatives since this book was published, the key ideas and issues maintain relevance.

Comprehensiveness

This textbook provides the reader with philosophical and legislative underpinnings of the assessment process, but readers would need to look elsewhere for more specific content about the process of actually doing an assessment.

Durability

A revised edition would on the surface make this seem more durable, that is, updating the legislation and examples from court cases. Nevertheless, the specific emphasis on including the views of service users and carers is consistent with current social work thinking in the UK.

Transferability

While specific reference is made to English legislation and court cases, the key ideas have wider applicability.

Learning exercises

Two learning exercises are provided at the end of the assessment chapter to further develop student learning.

Recommended further reading

Not provided.

Outstanding features

This textbook is very clear about the professional dilemmas that readily emerge while conducting assessments, especially the contradictions of anti-oppressive practice and professional responsibilities enshrined in legislation.

Shortcomings

Lack of detail about the process of conducting assessments.

Textbook

The Blackwell encyclopaedia of social work (2000) Oxford: Blackwell Publishers.[57]

Editor

Martin Davies.

Editor's affiliation at time of publication

Martin Davies is Professor of Social Work at the University of East Anglia, England.

Edition
First edition.

Cost
£17.99.

Intended audience
According to the blurb on the back cover, "The Blackwell Encyclopaedia of Social Work offers an essential starting point for anyone wanting to understand the place of social work in society today". The preface suggests that potential readers may include social work educators, students and practitioners, as well as interested readers from outside social work.

Number of pages – total
412 including List of Contributors, References and Indexes of Names and Contents (pp 381-412) plus Preface, Lexicon and Lists of Tables and Figures (pp v-xviii).

Number of pages – assessment
There are three separate entries on assessment, totalling 6 pages:
- Assessment in childcare, by Sonia Jackson, pp 20-1
- Assessment in community care, by Leonne Griggs, pp 22-3
- Assessment in work with offenders, by Hazel Kemshall and Charlotte Knight, pp 23-5.

Definitions of assessment
The following definitions are provided:

> *Assessment* is the process that controls the nature, direction and scope of social work interventions. It is particularly important in work with children because of its potential to initiate or influence life-changing decisions in relation to vulnerable individuals....

> There are two main aspects of assessment in child care: the first is concerned with decision making, the second with outcomes. (Jackson, 2000, p 20)

Assessment in community care involves the formation of a judgement concerning the needs of an adult which may result in their requirements being met by social care provision.

The aim of community care assessment is for a client's needs to be ascertained so that an individualized package of care can be provided. (Griggs, 2000, p 22)

Assessment can be described as a process of professional judgement or appraisal of the situation, circumstances and behaviour of the offender. (Kemshall and Knight, 2000, p 23)

Timing of assessment

The timing of assessment varies according to the setting:

Assessment is not a one-off activity, but a continuous process which needs to take account of changing family circumstances and the child's growing capacity to take an active part in decision making. Time is needed for the social worker to assess the potential strengths of the family and its ability to change. On the other hand, there are strong arguments for setting firm boundaries to avoid the phenomenon of drift in care. (Jackson, 2000, p 21)

There is an initial screening that determines the level of assessment, whether the presenting problem is appropriate to the agency, and whether eligibility criteria are applicable. The community care assessment ... shows the client's position at a certain point in time and results in the formulation of a care plan that is implemented and monitored to ensure that changing needs continue to be met appropriately. (Griggs, 2000, p 22)

Assessment ... is one of the key tasks of the probation service at point of sentence, during community supervision, and for early release from custody. (Kemshall and Knight, 2000, p 23)

Theoretical underpinnings

Explicit discussions of the theoretical underpinnings of assessment are not included. A reference is provided for the theoretical bases for the Looking After Children materials (published by the Department of Health in the mid-1990s), and mention is made that assessment of offenders has moved from "the traditional psychoanalytic and diagnostic approach ... to those criminogenic factors which research has indicated are associated with offending" (Kemshall and Knight, 2000, p 23).

Information obtained during the assessment process

Information obtained in assessments using the Looking After Children materials includes:

- health
- education
- identity
- family and social relationships
- emotional and behavioural development
- social presentation
- self-care skills.

Information obtained in community care assessments should include the following in order to "construct a comprehensive picture of the client's needs, strengths, limitations and existing support structures" (Griggs, 2000, p 22):

- health needs
- physical and mental capacity
- emotional needs
- financial support
- addictions
- suitability of living environment
- occupational requirements
- carer support
- stresses
- risk factors.

Information obtained for assessments of offenders should include factors that research has demonstrated have an association with offending including:

- age
- gender
- previous convictions

- anti-social attitudes
- aggressive behaviours
- accommodation
- unemployment
- peer group networks.

Risk assessment

Risk is primarily discussed in respect of assessing offenders.

Multidisciplinary assessment

Not discussed in these entries. Elsewhere there are sections on 'Interagency work', 'Interdisciplinary practice' and 'Interprofessional practice'.

Involvement of users and carers in the process

Both children and their carers should be involved in the assessment of child care and for community care. It is noted that this is a particularly British emphasis, especially in relation to including children in the process:

> It is a legal requirement in Britain, as well as good practice, that children should be encouraged and enabled to express their ideas about their own situation and where they should live, an aspect of child care that was seriously neglected in the past and is still absent from discussion in much of the US literature. (Jackson, 2000, p 20)

Explicit involvement of service users and the families in assessments of offenders is not discussed. Rather, consultation with other agencies is considered an important aspect of the assessment process.

User and carer perspectives of the assessment process

Not included.

Evidence bases

It is noted that the Looking After Children materials and current approaches to assessing offenders were developed in response to issues identified in research. However, legislative requirements rather than empirical bases are cited as the basis for community care assessments.

Inclusion of case studies
No case studies are included.

Anti-discriminatory/anti-oppressive practice
Only one entry (assessment of offenders) notes the need for principles of anti-discriminatory practice to underpin the assessment process in order to promote equality.

Languages other than English and use of interpreters
Not mentioned.

Legislation/legal frameworks
The entry on assessment in childcare refers to the Children Act 1989. Entries on assessment in community care and of offenders note that the assessment process requires knowledge of the relevant legislation, and, as the entry on offenders notes, the process of assessment may change to reflect changes in legislation and policy.

Accuracy
The entry on assessment in childcare was written prior to the Department of Health's (2000) *Framework for the assessment of children in need and their families.*

Comprehensiveness
Each of the three above mentioned entries provides a brief introduction in about 1,000 words to the aims and nature of assessment in their respective fields of practice. Readers wanting information on how to conduct an assessment would need to look elsewhere, but recommended further reading is provided (see below).

Durability
By focusing on general concepts rather than specific legislation, policies or service providers, the entries will not date rapidly unless there is a major reorganisation of social work within the UK to something where the major groupings of social workers are not in children and families, community care and probation/criminal justice social work.

Transferability

This book was written particularly for the UK policy and practice context, in which assessments of children and families, of offenders, and for community care are governed by separate legislation, and usually conducted by separate staff groups.

Recommended further reading

Each entry recommends three additional books and/or articles for readers wanting further information about assessment.

Learning exercises

Not provided.

Outstanding features

The reader is made aware in just seven pages that assessment is not a singular concept, and that the process may differ considerably between client groups.

Shortcomings

By focusing on assessment in three particular settings, the reader is not provided with an overview of assessment in social work more generally that can be applied to other situations and settings.

Textbook

Social work: Critical theory and practice (2002) London: Sage Publications.[66]

Author

Jan Fook.

Author's affiliation at time of publication

Jan Fook is Professor and Director of the Centre for Professional Development at La Trobe University, Australia.

Edition

First edition.

Cost
£17.99.

Intended audience
According to the back cover, this book "will be essential reading for practitioners and students on qualifying and post-qualifying social work courses".

Number of pages – total
179 including References and Index (pp 169-79) plus Contents and Preface.

Number of pages – assessment
There are 11 pages in Chapter 9: Problem conceptualisation and assessment, pp 115-31.

Key headings within the chapter on assessment
- Criticisms of traditional notions of assessment and problems
- An alternative approach: Assessment as 'construction of professional narratives'
- Problematising
- Enabling the appropriate climate and process
- Research orientation and strategies
- Politics and context
- Integrated and changing nature of constructing personal narratives
- Reframing major concepts and language
- The main elements of a professional narrative
- Service user perspectives/story
- The perspectives of other players
- Contexts and changes
- How the narrative will be interpreted and enacted in the professional context of the worker
- Strategies
- Ethnographic and observational techniques
- Reflexive methods
- Other unobtrusive methods.

Definitions of assessment

While acknowledging more traditional definitions of assessment, Fook proposes:

> A new approach to the understanding and practice of assessment making involves a broad recognition that the act of assessing involves creating a set of meanings which function discursively. ... In reformulating the idea and practice of assessment, therefore, we need to allow for multiple and changing understandings which are contextually based and may be contradictory. We also need to acknowledge that the assessment made may primarily represent the perspective of the professional worker making it. Assessment making, in this sense, is no more or less than the professional worker constructing his or her own narrative of the problem situation. (Fook, 2002, p 118)

Timing of assessment

Not specified.

Theoretical underpinnings

Postmodern and critical thinking is proposed to facilitate the construction of professional narratives that seek to work in favour of service users.

Information obtained during the assessment process

In addition to interviews with service users, information may come from a range of sources, including observation and written or visual documents. Rather than 'problems', it is proposed that the focus should be on 'situations', 'contexts' and 'circumstances'.

Risk assessment

That social workers might undertake risk assessments is mentioned but there is no further discussion as to what this means or what issues may be associated with this.

Multidisciplinary assessment

Not discussed.

Involvement of users and carers in the process

While the involvement of service users and carers is considered crucial, a distinction is made between obtaining maximum exchange of information and maximum agreement between professionals and clients.

User and carer perspectives of the assessment process

Although the need for social workers to understand the lived experiences of service users is emphasised, this is not explicitly discussed in respect of the assessment process.

Evidence bases

While a range of academic literature is drawn upon, there is no explicit discussion about previous research findings. The reflexive methodology is proposed as a research strategy for making professional assessments.

Inclusion of case studies

Some brief examples are included in the main text of the chapter on assessment.

Anti-discriminatory/anti-oppressive practice

Although the terms 'anti-discriminatory' and 'anti-oppressive' practice are not mentioned, issues of race and gender are discussed in the chapter on assessment.

Languages other than English and use of interpreters

Not mentioned.

Legislation/legal frameworks

Not mentioned.

Accuracy

The emphasis on working in partnership with service users and carers is consistent with current policy and practice in the UK.

Comprehensiveness

The chapter on assessment assumes some knowledge of conventional social work assessment. Readers wanting introductory information on the assessment process would need to look elsewhere.

Durability

This is one of a growing number of social work textbooks that make explicit links with postmodern thinking, and as such proposes a perspective that is not likely to become out of fashion in the near future.

Transferability

Although the author is Australian (and the book was written in Australia), she draws considerably on recent social work literature from the UK.

Recommended further reading

Not included.

Learning exercises

These are included throughout the chapter on assessment.

Outstanding features

The assessment chapter goes beyond the basics, and strives to make connections between assessment, reflexive practice and research.

Shortcomings

The chapter assumes a beginning level of knowledge about the assessment process.

Textbook

Direct social work practice: Theory and skills (2002) Pacific Grove, CA: Brooks/Cole Publishing.[65]

Authors

Dean H. Hepworth, Ronald H. Rooney and Jo Ann Larsen.

Authors' affiliations at time of publication

Dean H. Hepworth is Professor Emeritus of Social Work at the University of Utah and Arizona State University, USA.

Ronald H. Mooney is Professor of Social Work at the University of Minnesota, USA.

Jo Ann Larsen is in private practice in Salt Lake City, USA, having previously taught in the school of social work at the University of Utah, USA.

Edition
Sixth edition.

Cost
£24.99.

Intended audience
This textbook is aimed at new social work students, especially those who have yet to undertake practice in an agency setting. According to the back cover, this book "provides learning experiences that are as close to real-life practice as you can get before stepping into the professional realm".

Number of pages – total
600 plus Contents and Preface (pp v-xxiii), References (pp R1-R31), Author Index (pp A1-A9) and Subject Index (pp S1-S15).

Number of pages – assessment
There are four chapters, totalling 140 pages, focusing on assessment:

Chapter 8: Multidimensional assessment, pp 187-217.

Chapter 9: Assessing intrapersonal and environmental systems, pp 219-58.

Chapter 10: Assessing family functioning in diverse family and cultural contexts, pp 259-98.

Chapter 11: Forming and assessing social work groups, pp 299-326.

Key headings within the chapters on assessment
Chapter 8: Multidimensional assessment
- Defining assessment: process and product
- Assessment and diagnosis

- Emphasizing strengths in assessments
- Sources of information
- The multidimensionality of assessment
- Written assessments
- Summary
- Internet resources.

Chapter 9: Assessing intrapersonal and environmental systems
- The interaction of multiple systems in human problems
- The intrapersonal systems
- Biophysical functioning
- Assessing use and abuse of alcohol and drugs
- Assessing cognitive/perceptual functioning
- Assessing emotional functioning
- Assessing affective disorders
- Assessing behavior functioning
- Assessing motivation
- Assessing cultural factors
- Assessing environmental systems
- Summary
- Internet resources.

Chapter 10: Assessing family functioning in diverse family and cultural contexts
- The evolution of family systems
- Family stressors
- Defining family
- A systems framework for assessing family functioning
- Systems impinging upon family functioning
- Family homeostasis
- Family rules
- Dimensions of family assessment
- Summary
- Internet resources.

Chapter 11: Forming and assessing social work groups
- Classification of groups
- Formation of treatment groups

- Assessing group processes
- Task groups
- Summary
- Internet resources.

Definitions of assessment

Assessment is defined as:

> ... a fluid and dynamic process that involves receiving, analysing and synthesizing new information as it emerges during the entire course of a given case. (Hepworth et al, 2002, p 188)

Timing of assessment

Assessment is an ongoing process, which continues until termination.

Theoretical underpinnings

The four assessment chapters elaborate on how systems theory can be used to underpin the assessment process.

Information obtained during the assessment process

Lists of questions are provided in relation to various types of assessment and the reader is referred to numerous standardised assessment tools. There is an emphasis on assessing both strengths and problems.

Risk assessment

Risk assessment is discussed in particular respect of suicide.

Multidisciplinary assessment

There is recognition that social workers may be only one of a range of disciplines contributing to an assessment but there is no discussion of the implications of multidisciplinary assessment.

Involvement of users and carers in the process

While there is brief mention of the need for client self-determination, assessment is very much portrayed as an activity conducted by professional social workers.

User and carer perspectives of the assessment process
Not included.

Evidence bases
Research evidence is explicitly discussed in several places.

Inclusion of case studies
Numerous case studies are included, ranging in length from brief scenarios to detailed written assessment reports.

Anti-discriminatory/anti-oppressive practice
There is no explicit mention of the terms 'anti-discriminatory' or 'anti-oppressive' practice. Nevertheless, there is extensive discussion of the need to understand cultural differences, especially those associated with race and ethnicity. Several examples of differences in culture between ethnic groups in North America are discussed. There is some discussion of issues of gender in relation to some case studies.

Languages other than English and use of interpreters
A number of issues are discussed in relation to clients whose first language is not English. These include the possibility of less expressive communication and clients being less able to articulate their problems in English. It is suggested that social workers need to speak slowly in simple terms and allow more time for clients to think and respond to questions. Use of interpreters is discussed briefly, including signing interpreters for deaf clients.

Legislation/legal frameworks
There is brief mention of the need for social workers to take account of legal mandates but no specific legislation is mentioned.

Accuracy
Recent research is cited but the four chapters on assessment reflect a greater emphasis on clinical social work in North America compared to a greater emphasis than on statutory social work in the UK. Some current emphases in UK social work, such as risk assessment, receive little mention.

Comprehensiveness
In addition to generalised information on assessment, there are chapters concerned with assessing families and groups, and significant portions of chapters concerned with assessing physical and mental health and substance misuse. However, readers wanting to locate assessment within UK policy and practice emphases would need to obtain this information elsewhere.

Durability
As this text discusses generalised concepts rather than addressing particular policies and legislation, it is not likely to date rapidly.

Transferability
This textbook is written for the North American market, where the philosophical underpinnings and emphases differ somewhat from those from within the UK. For example, there is considerable emphasis on client depression.

Recommended further reading
A list of Internet resources, including articles and assessment tools, is included in each chapter.

Learning exercises
Not included.

Outstanding features
This textbook assumes little prior knowledge about the assessment process and takes the reader through the various steps, including what sorts of questions they might ask, what other forms of data they might use, and what a written assessment might look like. The inclusion of separate chapters on assessing families and groups is helpful, as it enables the reader to understand the differences between assessing families and groups compared with assessing individuals.

Shortcomings
There are different emphases from those that predominate in UK policy and practice.

Textbook
Social work practice: Assessment, planning, intervention and review (2003)
Exeter: Learning Matters.[40]

Authors
Jonathan Parker and Greta Bradley.

Authors' affiliations at time of publication
Jonathan Parker is Head of Social Work at the University of Hull, England.

Greta Bradley is Senior Lecturer in Social Work at the University of Hull, England.

Edition
First edition.

Cost
£14.00.

Intended audience
First-year social work students on an undergraduate degree programme. Explicit mention is made of the new social work degree that was introduced in 2003 and of training requirements, but there is no recognition that the training requirements are those that have been specified for England and that these are not identical to those for students in Northern Ireland, Scotland or Wales.

Number of pages – total
148 including References and Index (pp 137-48) plus Introduction (pp i-xi).

Number of pages – assessment
There are two chapters, totalling 60 pages, focusing on assessment:

Chapter 1: Understanding assessment in social work, pp 1-37.

Chapter 2: Tools and diagrammatic aids to assessment, pp 39-61.

Key headings within the chapters on assessment

Chapter 1: Understanding assessment in social work practice

- Introduction
- What is assessment? Definitional perspectives
- Assessment: art or science?
- Assessment types in social work
- Assessment as an ongoing, fluid and dynamic process
- Single event/time-specific formulations
- Levels of assessment in social work
- The purpose of assessment in social work
- Strengths and social exclusion
- Skills in assessment
- Characteristics and features of assessments
- Specific uses of assessment with children and families and in care management
- Framework for assessment of children in need and their families
- Care management and assessment
- Background to care management
- Care management and the process of assessment
- Eligibility criteria and fair access to care services
- Chapter summary.

Chapter 2: Tools and diagrammatic aids to assessment

- Introduction
- Genograms
- The uses of genograms
- Symbols used in developing genograms
- Genograms in family therapy
- Ecomaps
- How to construct an ecomap
- Culturagrams
- Culturagrams in working with abuse
- Flow diagrams and life road maps
- Using road maps
- Chapter summary.

Definitions of assessment

The following definition is provided:

> The *Oxford English Dictionary* sees assessment in terms of judging or valuing the worth of something. This is an indication of a skilled activity by someone who is competent to judge between things of different value. It implies the use of standards against which something can be appraised. This certainly appears to be the case in many social work assessments. However, it leaves out the interactive and human contexts which also feature in social work assessments. The definition suggests that there are right and wrong situations or good and bad values; a suggestion that, in social work, demands critical appraisal.

> A balanced approach would suggest that social work assessment is both an art and a science since it involves wisdom, skills, appreciation of diversity, and systematically applied knowledge in practice. (Parker and Bradley, 2003, pp 3-4)

Timing of assessment

Assessment may be time-limited in relation to a specific issue or may be an ongoing process.

Theoretical underpinnings

A range of theoretical perspectives are identified.

Information obtained during the assessment process

It is noted that assessment is not a singular concept or process, and therefore the information collected and analysed will vary according to the situation. Examples of the process in relation to the *Framework for the assessment of children in need and their families* and assessments of adults that take into account the NHS and Community Care Act 1990 and the Single Shared Assessment are included.

Chapter Two provides details of a number of assessment tools, including genograms, ecomaps, culturagrams, flow diagrams and life road maps.

Risk assessment

This is mentioned briefly and discussed more fully in a subsequent chapter.

Multidisciplinary assessment

Multidisciplinary assessment is discussed in relation to the requirements of the *Framework for the assessment of children in need and their families*, and for the Single Assessment Process for older persons.

Involvement of users and carers in the process

There is brief explicit mention of involving service users and carers in the assessment process, and it is implicit in several of the case examples.

User and carer perspectives of the assessment process

The social worker's view as to what a service user's perspective might be on the assessment process is part of a case study.

Evidence bases

Explicit mentions of research evidence are included.

Inclusion of case studies

There are numerous case examples included throughout these chapters on assessment.

Anti-discriminatory/anti-oppressive practice

In Chapter One, the section 'Values and diversity in assessment' discusses the concepts, but does not use the labels 'anti-discriminatory' or 'anti-oppressive' practice. Chapter Two includes details on using a 'culturagram', which can assist gaining understanding of the meaning and impact of culture on individuals and families.

Languages other than English and use of interpreters

The potential for communication difficulties with people whose first language is not English is briefly discussed, but use of interpreters is not one of the strategies mentioned for facilitating communication.

Legislation/legal frameworks

Specific (English) legislation is provided, along with mapping of content onto the National Occupational Standards.

Accuracy

This textbook refers to social work literature, current legislation and policy contexts.

Comprehensiveness

This textbook provides the reader with an overview of the current literature, legislation and policy contexts for social work assessment in England. Readers wanting more detailed information on a specific approach to assessment are guided to further reading.

Durability

As there is extensive emphasis on current policy and legislative contexts, this text has the potential to become outdated in a relatively short time-frame.

Transferability

The close fit with English legislation and requirements limits transferability of this textbook both outside the UK and within UK to countries other than England.

Recommended further reading

Each chapter includes recommendations for further reading.

Learning exercises

Learning activities are included in each chapter.

Outstanding features

These chapters provide an overview of the current literature on assessment, with explicit mention of differences in relation to many of the topics discussed.

Shortcomings

Key shortcomings of this textbook are the potential lack of durability and absence of acknowledgement that this book relates specifically to the requirements for social work education and practice in England.

Textbook

Constructive social work: Towards a new practice (2000) Basingstoke: Macmillan.[61]

Authors

Nigel Parton and Patrick O'Byrne.

Authors' affiliations at time of publication

Nigel Parton was Professor of Child Care and Director of the Centre for Applied Social Studies at the University of Huddersfield, England.

Patrick O'Byrne was Senior Lecturer in Social Work at the University of Huddersfield, England from 1979 to 1999.

Edition

First edition.

Cost

£16.99.

Intended audience

According to the back cover, "This book will prove invaluable for all students and practitioners in social work, counselling and other human service professions".

Number of pages – total

246 including Appendices, Further Reading, Bibliography and Index (pp 188-246) plus Contents and Acknowledgements (pp v-ix).

Number of pages – assessment

There are 18 pages in Chapter 8: Constructive assessment, pp 134-51.

Key headings within chapters on assessment
- Constructive assessment
- Theoretic issues
- The content of assessments
- Risk.

Definitions of assessment
The following definition is provided:

> Social work assessments, ... especially in statutory agencies, are usually written formally and are for the use of others in authority. This assessment work is essentially the work of *making judgments, so that decision-making can be better informed.* (Parton and O'Byrne, 2000, p 134)

Timing of assessment
Assessment is ongoing and happens on a continuous basis as an aspect of intervention rather than something that precedes intervention.

Theoretical underpinnings
"Constructive assessment" is part of an overall approach proposed by the authors, which they call "constructive social work". It is an approach that seeks to integrate social theory with social work practice. The various theoretical bases for constructive assessment are explicitly discussed.

Information obtained during the assessment process
Rather than focusing on people's weaknesses or deficits, constructive assessment emphasises their strengths and abilities. Issues are contextualised within a narrative of lived experiences, rather than problems being the sole focus of information obtained during the assessment process.

Risk assessment
The final six-page section of the chapter is headed 'Risk'. Noting that this is often perceived as problematic by social workers and their managers, Parton and O'Byrne suggest a more positive approach to assessing risk. This section discusses both the content (what information is sought) and process (how information is sought) in a risk assessment.

Multidisciplinary assessment

Not discussed.

Involvement of users and carers in the process

Facilitating the active involvement of service users and carers is an essential aspect of constructive assessment.

User and carer perspectives of the assessment process

Parton and O'Byrne in general emphasise the need for social workers to understand the lived experiences of service users, although they do not explicitly discuss this in respect of the assessment process.

Evidence bases

The authors draw on the writings of several notable authors in social work, social theory and cognate disciplines. However, there is little explicit discussion of research evidence.

Inclusion of case studies

Not included.

Anti-discriminatory/anti-oppressive practice

Although the terms 'anti-discriminatory practice' and 'anti-oppressive practice' are not used, the need for acknowledging differences and openness about culture and values is discussed, and the underlying philosophy of the chapter on assessment is consistent with the concept of anti-discriminatory practice.

Languages other than English and use of interpreters

Not mentioned.

Legislation/legal frameworks

There is just one mention of a specific piece of legislation, but the general requirements of statutory social work are discussed throughout the chapter on assessment.

Accuracy

Inclusion of a section on 'risk' reflects current concerns and dialogues about assessment in the UK.

Comprehensiveness

This textbook provides the reader with a philosophical and conceptual approach to assessment, with some concrete suggestions around content.

Durability

The material in the assessment chapter is unlikely to date rapidly.

Transferability

Although written within the UK policy and practice context, the chapter on assessment would be readily accessible to social work students and practitioners elsewhere.

Recommended further reading

There is a six-page section on further reading at the end of the book, but this is delineated into sections concerned with specific populations and problems. There are no specific recommendations for further reading on the topic of assessment.

Learning exercises

Not provided.

Outstanding features

This is a text that is strong on theory and is likely to challenge even some experienced social workers.

Shortcomings

Beginning social work students may feel the need to read other texts that provide more concrete details on the process of setting up and conducting an assessment to complement their reading of this text. The authors discuss several theorists (including Lacan and Winnicott) but provide no background on these writers. As such, this textbook may be better suited to undergraduate students in later years of study or postgraduate students rather than beginning undergraduates.

Textbook
Social work skills: A practice handbook (2000) Buckingham: Open University Press.[70]

Author
Pamela Trevithick.

Author's affiliation at time of publication
Pamela Trevithick works as a practitioner and consultant in child protection and as a Lecturer in Social Work at the University of Bristol, England.

Edition
First edition.

Cost
£17.99.

Intended audience
This book is primarily aimed at UK social work students undertaking practice learning.

Number of pages – total
216 including Appendices, References and Index (pp 177-216) plus Contents and Acknowledgements.

Number of pages – assessment
There is one chapter of 19 pages on assessment, Chapter 3: The importance of communication, listening and assessment skills, pp 50-68.

Key headings within the chapter on assessment
- Common problems
- Solutions and services
- Communication skills
- Language
- Non-verbal forms of communication
- Observation
- Listening skills

- Organizing and planning skills
- Forming decisions and making judgements
- The purpose of assessment
- Practice emphasis
- Need-led versus resource-led assessments
- Evaluating outcomes
- User feedback
- Conclusion.

Definitions of assessment

It is noted that:

> The fact that assessments serve different purposes means that they can encompass different social work approaches and perspectives, give weight to certain factors or problems more than others, and propose different solutions. (Trevithick, 2000, p 62)

Timing of assessment

It is noted that while some authors propose assessment as a task that precedes intervention, others propose that assessment should be an on-going process. No suggestion is made as to which of these approaches should be considered preferable.

Theoretical underpinnings

The chapter is more of a survey of the literature on assessment than a work that draws on or develops specific theoretical perspectives on assessment.

Information obtained during the assessment process

A wide range of different reasons for undertaking assessments are noted, with the understanding that the information sought and from whom it is sought will vary according to the purpose of the assessment. However, specific details are not provided.

Risk assessment

Although the section 'Forming decisions and making judgements' does not mention the word 'risk', the issues contained in this section pertain to the concept of risk assessment.

Multidisciplinary assessment

Legislative requirements for some multidisciplinary assessments are noted. Issues or tensions that can emerge in multidisciplinary assessments are discussed.

Involvement of users and carers in the process

While the involvement of service users and carers in the assessment process is discussed, it is noted that there is considerable disagreement in the literature as to the extent to which service users should be involved in decision making.

User and carer perspectives of the assessment process

A section on 'User feedback' encourages practitioners actively to seek feedback from clients about services.

A piece of research demonstrating how service users may misunderstand common words and phrases used by social workers is also presented in the chapter on assessment.

Evidence bases

A number of empirical studies are explicitly discussed.

Inclusion of case studies

Some practice examples are included in the chapter.

Anti-discriminatory/anti-oppressive practice

This is discussed in relation to assessment in one paragraph.

Languages other than English and use of interpreters

Not mentioned.

Legislation/legal frameworks

Some specific English legislation is referred to in respect of the policy context in which assessment occurs.

Accuracy

There have been some changes since this text was written. For example, the Department of Health's *Framework for the assessment of children in need and their families* is no longer a draft document, and the guidelines for social work education set by the former Central Council on Education and Training in Social Work are in the process of being replaced.

Comprehensiveness
The chapter is very much a survey of the literature on assessment rather than guidance on how to conduct assessments.

Durability
As new assessment frameworks become available, and the new social work degrees are implemented, some updating is likely to be required.

Transferability
A somewhat explicit UK basis makes this text less transferable to other countries than texts that are less tied to a UK context.

Recommended further reading
Readers who wish to read more of Watzlawick et al's (1974) distinction of first- and second-order change are referred to the relevant page numbers. No other further reading is recommended.

Learning exercises
Not provided.

Outstanding features
The reader is left in no doubt that assessment is not a singular concept and that there are numerous disputes in the literature about assessment processes.

Shortcomings
Students wanting specific details about assessments in various contexts will need to look elsewhere.

Appendix 2:
Textbooks on assessment

Textbook
Social assessment theory and practice: A multi-disciplinary framework
(1998) Aldershot: Ashgate Publishing Limited.[75]

Author
Derek Clifford.

Author's affiliation at time of publication
Derek Clifford is Senior Lecturer in Social Work at Liverpool John
Moores University, England.

Edition
First edition.

Cost
£50.65.

Intended audience
This textbook is aimed at practitioners who conduct social assessments,
including social workers.

Number of pages – total
289 including References and Subject and Author Indexes (pp 245-89)
plus Contents, List of Figures, Preface, Autobiographical Notes and
Acknowledgements, and Notes on Terminology (pp v-xx).

Section and chapter titles
Part 1: Critical auto/biography: social theory for social assessment
- Chapter 1: Values and methodology
- Chapter 2: Taking social difference seriously
- Chapter 3: Reflexivity: personal involvement and responsibility

- Chapter 4: Historical location
- Chapter 5: Interacting social systems: the personal and the structural
- Chapter 6: Power.

Part 2: Critical auto/biography: developing methods and dialogues in practice
- Chapter 7: Social assessment and multi-professional practice
- Chapter 8: Assessing needs, risks and strengths
- Chapter 9: Children and families
- Chapter 10: Mental health and distress
- Chapter 11: Older people
- Chapter 12: Disabled people.

Part 3: Conclusion
- Chapter 13: Towards effective social work assessment.

Definitions of assessment

Clifford writes that:

> I am using 'social assessment' in a broad sense to refer to social as distinct from psychological or medical assessment – this is, assessment which is centred on social explanation. … Social assessment may cover assessment of social needs on a community-wide or even larger scale, but here I am concerned mainly with social assessment of individuals and small groups. (Clifford, 1998, p xix)

Timing of assessment

An assessment reflects a situation at a point in history, but should be reviewed regularly as long as professional intervention continues.

Theoretical underpinnings

Drawing on a broad range of social theory, in the first half of the textbook, Clifford proposes a 'critical auto/biography' framework of assessment and then demonstrates its utility in respect of a range of service-user groups in the remainder of the textbook.

Information obtained during the assessment process

For Clifford, the assessor is a social researcher who uses a range of data collection methods to obtain relevant data from a range of sources. In addition to assessors collecting data about service users, they are encouraged to reflect critically on the social differences between themselves and those they are assessing in order to gain further insights about service users.

Risk assessment

There is one chapter titled 'Assessing needs, risks and strengths'. There are numerous mentions of risk assessment elsewhere in this textbook.

Multidisciplinary assessment

There is one chapter titled 'Social assessment and multi-professional practice'. There are numerous mentions of multidisciplinary working elsewhere in this textbook.

Involvement of users and carers in the process

The critical auto/biographical method is proposed as a method of gaining greater insight into the lives of service users and carers. It is important that the voices of service users and carers be given prominence in an assessment, but the extent to which users and carers are involved in the process is not always clear.

User and carer perspectives of the assessment process

Although actual examples of user and carer perspectives on the assessment process are not provided, the reader is continually encouraged to try to understand what it is that service users and carers are experiencing.

Evidence bases

Clifford draws on an extensive breadth of literature both from within and beyond the discipline of social work. Much of this literature is theoretical, but at times he discusses the adequacy of empirical literature.

Inclusion of case studies

One case study involving a family with several members is discussed in detail in relation to the needs of different family members in several chapters.

Anti-discriminatory/anti-oppressive practice

Clifford is not keen on the term 'anti-oppressive' practice, preferring to write about social division. This is discussed throughout the textbook, as well as being the focus of one chapter.

Languages other than English and use of interpreters

Not mentioned.

Legislation/legal frameworks

Some specific English legislation is mentioned, but readers would need to look elsewhere for details about these pieces of legislation.

Accuracy

Although there have been some changes in social work policy and practice contexts in the UK since the textbook was published in 1998, issues of current prominence such as service-user involvement are given considerable emphasis.

Comprehensiveness

This is an advanced textbook, which assumes that the reader has some familiarity with disciplines such as social theory, sociology and psychology. It is a challenging text for graduate students and practitioners. First year undergraduates or readers wanting introductory information on the assessment process would need to look elsewhere.

Durability

The textbook is unlikely to date rapidly, given increasing interest in narrative and auto/biographical approaches in social work and some cognate disciplines.

Transferability

Although grounded in social work, this textbook is not limited to promoting a social work perspective, and may well appeal to advanced practitioners in a range of cognate disciplines.

Recommended further reading

Not provided.

Learning exercises

Several questions are put to the reader at the end of each chapter.

Outstanding features

This is an original and challenging book, which is intellectually rigorous and demonstrates the benefits of social workers having a good grounding in social theory, and how this can enhance practice skills.

Shortcomings

Very expensive.

Textbook

Good practice in risk assessment and management 1 (1996) London: Jessica Kingsley Publishers.[73]

Editors

Hazel Kemshall and Jacki Pritchard.

Editors' affiliations at time of publication

Hazel Kemshall is a lecturer in probation studies at the University of Birmingham.

Jacki Pritchard is an accredited practice teacher who works as a freelance trainer and consultant in England and Northern Ireland.

Edition

First edition.

Cost

£17.95.

Intended audience

According to the back cover, this is "a book which every practitioner, manager and student should be able to draw from" and is published as part of a series that "explores topics of current concern to professionals working in social work".

Number of pages
210 including List of Contributors, Subject Index and Author Index (pp. 198-210) plus Contents (two pages).

Chapter titles
- Introduction by Hazel Kemshall and Jacki Pritchard
- Chapter 1: Risking legal repercussions, by David Carson
- Chapter 2: Risk assessment in child protection work, by Brian Corby
- Chapter 3: Children with disabilities, by Philippa Russell
- Chapter 4: Framework of risk assessment and management for older people, by Jane Lawson
- Chapter 5: Risk and older people, by Rosemary Littlechild and John Blakeney
- Chapter 6: Risk for whom? Social work and people with physical disabilities, by Liz Ross and Jan Waterson
- Chapter 7: Risk management and people with mental health problems, by Tony Ryan
- Chapter 8: Risk work and mental health, by Ann Davis
- Chapter 9: Facts, fantasies and confusion: risks and substance use, by Ronno Griffiths and Jan Waterson
- Chapter 10: Offender risk and probation practice, by Hazel Kemshall
- Chapter 11: Sex offenders risk assessment, by Sue McEwan and Joe Sullivan
- Chapter 12: The risk of violence and aggression to social work and social care staff, by Brian Littlechild
- Chapter 13: Applying risk in practice: case studies and training material, by Avril Aust, Hazel Kemshall, Jane Lawson, Sue McEwan, Joe Sullivan, Jacki Pritchard and Tony Ryan.

Definition of assessment
Although assessment is not defined, the scope of risk assessment is. As the authors of one chapter note:

> Environmental, social, physical and emotional aspects need considering and the analysis should allow for beneficial as well as harmful outcomes. Risk assessment then becomes the task of estimating the

probability and size of known possible outcomes resulting from a complex interaction of known and unknown factors. (Ross and Waterson, 1994, p 81)

Timing of assessment

The timing and duration of assessments vary according to context as the various chapters show. In some contexts there may be an initial or preliminary assessment followed by a more detailed or long-term assessment should contact be ongoing. While some assessments may occur at a point of crisis, others are ongoing with decisions being made on a continual basis.

Theoretical underpinnings

The exchange model of assessment was mentioned in one chapter. Theoretical models of assessment are not explicit in the other chapters.

Information obtained during the assessment process

Some chapters include checklists of issues that should be explored in risk assessments.

Risk assessment

Risk assessment is the focus of this textbook.

Multidisciplinary assessment

Multidisciplinary assessment is mentioned in several chapters. It is noted that in some instances there are legislative requirements for more than one profession to be involved in an assessment.

Involvement of users and carers in the process

Several chapters explore the tension between involving service users and carers as much as possible and making professional assessments that contradict the desires of service users and carers.

User and carer perspectives of the assessment process

The authors of several chapters encourage readers to try to understand what it is like for service users to be assessed.

Evidence bases
The importance of basing risk assessments on research and not merely on unsubstantiated assumptions is emphasised in several chapters.

Inclusion of case studies
The final chapter includes 11 case studies. Several other chapters also include case studies.

Anti-discriminatory/anti-oppressive practice
Although the words 'anti-discriminatory' and 'anti-oppressive' practice are rarely used, the underlying principles underpin several of the chapters.

Languages other than English and use of interpreters
Not discussed.

Legislation/legal frameworks
One chapter focuses particularly on legislation and legal frameworks, and several other chapters include some discussion of these.

Accuracy
This book precedes the *Framework for the assessment of children in need and their families*, referring instead to the guidance which had been published in 1988.

Comprehensiveness
This textbook provides introductory information on risk assessment in a number of settings. However, readers would need to look elsewhere for specific content about the process of actually going about and doing an assessment.

Durability
Although this book is regarded by some social work educators as a seminal text, risk assessment is a developing component of social work and one might expect to see further developments in professional dialogues in future texts concerned with risk assessment.

Transferability
This textbook discusses risk assessment in a range of settings. However, many of the ideas transcend the particular settings that are the focus of the chapters they are discussed within.

Recommended further reading
Not included.

Learning exercises
The final chapter includes 11 case studies, several of which have questions for discussion.

Outstanding features
The reader gets a good feel for the similarities and differences in assessment practice between different service-user groups.

Shortcomings
This is a textbook that assumes that readers have some knowledge of the assessment process. Beginning social work students who are beginning to learn about assessment would need to supplement their reading of this text with readings from other sources.

Textbook
Good practice in risk assessment and management 2: Protection, rights and responsibilities (1997) London: Jessica Kingsley Publishers.[74]

Editors
Hazel Kemshall and Jacki Pritchard.

Editors' affiliations at time of publication
Hazel Kemshall is a lecturer in probation studies at the University of Birmingham.

Jacki Pritchard is an accredited practice teacher who works as a freelance trainer and consultant in England and Northern Ireland.

Edition
First edition.

Cost
£19.95.

Intended audience
According to the back cover, "this book will prove a useful tool to those working with risk in providing practical strategies for effective intervention" and is published as part of a series that "explores topics of current concern to professionals working in social work".

Number of pages
327 including List of Contributors, Subject Index and Author Index (pp 312-27) plus Contents (two pages).

Chapter titles
- Introduction by Hazel Kemshall and Jacki Pritchard
- Chapter 1: Improving judgement and appreciating biases within the risk assessment process, by Robert Strachan and Chris Tallant
- Chapter 2: Taking the risk? Assessing lesbian and gay carers, by Stephen Hicks
- Chapter 3: Making family placements: working with risks and building on strengths, by Anne van Meeuwen
- Chapter 4: Risk in adoption and fostering, by Sheila Byrne
- Chapter 5: One of the hardest jobs: attempting to manage risk in children's homes, by Hilary Owen
- Chapter 6: Vulnerable people taking risks: Older people and residential care, by Jacki Pritchard
- Chapter 7: People with learning difficulties: citizenship, personal development and the management of risk, by Bob Tindall
- Chapter 8: We can take it: young people and drug use, by Peter Argyll and Ben Cowderoy
- Chapter 9: Alcohol: the effects and risks for individuals, by Pamela Askham
- Chapter 10: Homelessness and mental health: risk assessment, by Sue Lipscombe
- Chapter 11: Risk, residential services and people with mental health needs, by Tony Ryan
- Chapter 12: Community care homicide inquiries and risk assessment, by Michael Howlett

- Chapter 13: Risk and prison suicide, by Alison Liebling
- Chapter 14: Teenage suicide and self-harm: assessing and managing risk, by Juliet Lyon
- Chapter 15: Risk and parole: issues in risk assessment for release, by Hazel Kemshall
- Chapter 16: Rights versus risks: issues in work with prisoners, by Brian Williams
- Chapter 17: Risk, domestic violence and probation practice, by Katherine Beattie
- Chapter 18: Throughcare practice, risk and contact with victims, by Peter Johnston
- Chapter 19: Risk: the role and responsibility of middle managers, by Christine Lawrie.

Definition of assessment
No definition of assessment is provided.

Timing of assessment
Although no timeframes are suggested, there are a few references to time restrictions in the 'real world', as well as the need to plan.

Theoretical underpinnings
Theoretical models of assessment are not made explicit.

Information obtained during the assessment process
Some chapters include checklists of issues that should be explored in risk assessments.

Risk assessment
Risk assessment is the focus of this textbook.

Multidisciplinary assessment
Working in multidisciplinary teams within and across agencies is discussed in a number of chapters.

Involvement of users and carers in the process

Some chapters explore the tension between involving service users and carers as much as possible and making professional assessments that contradict the desires of service users and carers.

User and carer perspectives of the assessment process

The authors of several chapters encourage readers to try to understand what it is like for service users to be assessed.

Evidence bases

The importance of basing risk assessments on research and not merely on unsubstantiated assumptions is emphasised in several chapters.

Inclusion of case studies

Most chapters include case studies.

Anti-discriminatory/anti-oppressive practice

Although the words 'anti-discriminatory' and 'anti-oppressive' practice are rarely used, the underlying principles underpin several of the chapters.

Languages other than English and use of interpreters

Not discussed.

Legislation/legal frameworks

There are mentions of legislation and legal frameworks in several chapters but no detailed discussion of these.

Accuracy

This book precedes the Department of Health's (2000) *Framework for the assessment of children in need and their families* and the setting of care standards by the various care councils.

Comprehensiveness

This is an advanced textbook with several of the chapters being aimed at unit managers or training staff rather than students or newly qualified practitioners. Readers would need to look elsewhere for specific content about the process of actually going about and doing an assessment.

Durability
Although this book is regarded by some social work educators as a seminal text, risk assessment is a developing component of social work and one might expect to see further developments in professional dialogues in future texts concerned with risk assessment.

Transferability
This textbook discusses risk assessment in a range of settings. However, many of the ideas transcend the particular settings that are the focus of the chapters they are discussed within.

Recommended further reading
Included in one chapter only.

Learning exercises
Two chapters include outlines of training sessions that could be run by training staff on risk assessment.

Outstanding features
This is a textbook in which experienced practitioners struggle with the very real dilemmas that they confront in a range of settings.

Shortcomings
This is a textbook that assumes that readers have some knowledge of the assessment process. Beginning social work students who are beginning to learn about assessment would need to supplement their reading of this text with readings from other sources.

Textbook
The art of assessment (1997) Birmingham: Venture Press.[71]

Author
Laura Middleton.

Author's affiliation at time of publication
Laura Middleton is Head of Social Work at the University of Central Lancashire, England.

Edition
First edition.

Cost
£10.99.

Intended audience
This textbook is part of a series of Practitioner Guides published on behalf of the British Association of Social Workers.

Number of pages
76 including References (p 76) plus Contents and Acknowledgements.

Chapter titles
- Introduction: a question of balance
- What is assessment?
- The dynamics of need, demand and special need
- Organisational agendas
- Inter-agency working
- Good and bad assessment
- Professional and management issues.

Definitions of assessment
The following definition is provided:

> Assessment is the analytical process by which decisions are made. In a social welfare context, it is a basis for planning what needs to be done to maintain or improve a person's situation, although it is not the plan itself. Still less is it the organisational arrangements which will be made to put the plan into operation, but the assessor will need to know that such arrangements are possible and acceptable before surrendering responsibility for the assessment. Assessment involves gathering and interpreting information in order to understand a person and their circumstances: the desirability and feasibility of change and the services and resources which are necessary to effect it. It involves making judgements based on information. (Middleton, 1997, p 5)

Timing of assessment

Assessment comes prior to planning and delivering services. It is noted that: "Assessments take time and cost money, and their numbers are consequently restricted by organisations" (Middleton, 1997, p 18).

Theoretical underpinnings

This textbook reflects the change in philosophy in the NHS and Community Care Act 1990 from resource-led to needs-led assessments, and discusses Bradshaw's typologies of need to some length.

Information obtained during the assessment process

The need to collect pertinent information is stressed, noting that not to impose such a restriction is intrusive, and can result in invasions of privacy and time wasting. Lists of possible domains for exploration are provided in relation to sources of stress, personal and practical resources, and coping mechanisms.

Risk assessment

Once data have been collected, one aspect of their analysis concerns the identification of risks.

Multidisciplinary assessment

One chapter (seven pages) is concerned with 'Inter-agency working', with a particular focus on working with the health sector. Concerns are expressed for clients, for whom the process may seem unduly complex and repetitive if a number of workers are asking them for the same or similar information.

Involvement of users and carers in the process

Assessment is portrayed as a professional activity, although the views of service users and carers need to be sought out. In relation to carers, it should not be assumed that they have a desire or ability to provide care.

User and carer perspectives of the assessment process

There are occasional mentions of how service users may experience situations, as perceived by professionals.

Evidence bases
There is little explicit discussion of research evidence.

Inclusion of case studies
Case examples are used.

Anti-discriminatory/anti-oppressive practice
Notwithstanding the organisational imperatives, anti-oppressive practice is promoted as an imperative.

Languages other than English and use of interpreters
Not mentioned.

Legislation/legal frameworks
The NHS and Community Care Act 1990 and the Children Act 1990 are referred to but not more recent legislation.

Accuracy
There have been considerable changes in policy and practice since this textbook was written. It was written when there was a Conservative government at Westminster, and prior to the introduction of the *Framework for the assessment of children in need and their families*.

Comprehensiveness
This textbook provides some introductory information about the assessment process and places it within organisational constraints and policy contexts.

Durability
While much of this textbook is still relevant, the policy context has changed somewhat since it was written.

Transferability
Although written particularly for the UK policy and practice context, this textbook does not rely on readers having a detailed understanding of the UK context.

Recommended further reading

Some recommendations for further reading are incorporated into the text.

Learning exercises

Not provided.

Outstanding features

This is a brief and very readable book, which readily engages the reader and encourages them to think about the broader contexts of practice.

Shortcomings

Assessment is considered only in relation to individuals and not other social groupings.

Textbook

Assessment in social work (2002) Basingstoke: Macmillan.[75]

Authors

Judith Milner and Patrick O'Byrne.

Authors' affiliations at time of publication

Judith Milner is a freelance therapist with the Northorpe Hall Trust Counselling Scheme and Associate Fellow at the School of Safety and Well-being at the University of Warwick, England.

Patrick O'Byrne is a freelance therapist with the Northorpe Hall Trust Counselling Scheme and a family mediator with the West Yorkshire Family Mediation Service, England.

Edition

Second edition.

Cost

£15.99.

Intended audience

According to the back cover, "This is an essential text for students of social work, qualified practitioners and social work educators who are committed to high-quality assessment practice".

Number of pages

214 including References and Index (pp 192-214) plus Contents, List of Tables and Figures, and Acknowledgements (pp v-ix).

Chapter titles

- Chapter 1: Introduction
- Chapter 2: From traditional practice to new complexities
- Chapter 3: Anti-oppressive practice
- Chapter 4: Decision outcomes and the assessment process
- Chapter 5: Selecting a map
- Chapter 6: A map of the ocean: psychodynamic approaches
- Chapter 7: An ordnance survey map: behavioural approaches
- Chapter 8: The handy tourist map: task-centred approach
- Chapter 9: The navigator's map: solution-focused approaches
- Chapter 10: A forecast map: narrative approaches
- Chapter 11: Making and finalising the judgement
- Chapter 12: Conclusion.

Definition of assessment

Rather than provide a definition, Milner and O'Byrne make the following observation about assessment:

> We see assessment as a journey for which social workers need to select the most appropriate map if they are to get to their destinations quickly and efficiently. We do not believe that assessment can be easily separated from intervention – change happens at all stages of the social work process – but we do think it dangerous to read a road map while driving. So we recommend that social workers familiarise themselves with a range of maps before planning the assessment journey. Should they get lost on the way or should the service user not meet them at the destination, they will then need to consult the maps again. (Milner and O'Byrne, 2002, p 4)

Milner and O'Byrne then go on to propose a five-stage framework for the assessment process:

1. *Preparation.* Deciding who to see, what data will be relevant, what the purpose is and the limits of the task are.
2. *Data collection.* People are met and engaged with, difference gaps are addressed, and empowerment and choice are safeguarded as we come to the task with respectful uncertainty and a research mentality.
3. *Weighing the data.* Current social and psychological theory and research findings that are part of every social worker's learning are drawn on to answer the questions 'Is there a problem?' and 'How serious is it?" ....
4. *Analysing the data.* One or more of the analytic maps are then used to interpret the data and to seek to gain an understanding of them in order to develop their ideas for intervention....
5. *Utilising the analysis.* This is the stage in which judgments are finalised.... (Milner and O'Byrne, 2002, p 6)

Timing of assessment

The authors note that while most writers propose that assessment is an ongoing process, there is little evidence to suggest that initial assessments are reviewed.

Theoretical underpinnings

Separate chapters are included on psychodynamic, behavioural, task-centred, solution-focused and narrative approaches to assessment.

Information obtained during the assessment process

Information is provided about the types of information that are emphasised by each of the various approaches to assessment, and how this can be obtained.

Risk assessment

There are numerous references to risk assessment throughout this textbook.

Multidisciplinary assessment
One section details some concerns about interagency assessments.

Involvement of users and carers in the process
The authors explicitly discuss tensions around the limits of service-user involvement. For example, it is noted that:

> Despite the principle that individuals should be allowed to assess the risks to themselves, ... should an elderly person be found to have died alone at home it is likely that social work will be found culpable. (Milner and O'Byrne, 2002, p 23)

User and carer perspectives of the assessment process
There is a very useful section on the complexities of evaluating service-user satisfaction.

Evidence bases
The adequacy of the research evidence to support the various approaches to assessment is explicitly discussed.

Inclusion of case studies
Case examples are used throughout the text.

Anti-discriminatory/anti-oppressive practice
An entire chapter (22 pages) focuses on anti-oppressive practice in assessment.

Languages other than English and use of interpreters
Not mentioned.

Legislation/legal frameworks
A five-page section (pp 14-18) considers the impact of legislation on the assessment process for English social workers.

Accuracy
This is a textbook that addresses the demands of the current policy and practice contexts of social work practice in the UK. Where these result in contradictions and dilemmas, the authors explicitly note these rather

than ignoring or minimising the issues that these may raise for social workers.

Comprehensiveness

The authors provide a framework for assessment and demonstrate its use with five distinct theoretical approaches to assessment. The framework, however, could be adapted by readers who are interested in exploring the utility of alternative theoretical approaches.

Durability

The authors themselves note a range of changes that impact on the assessment process since the first edition of this textbook was published in 1998, just four years prior to this edition. However, the guiding principles and frameworks that are provided for the reader are unlikely to date rapidly.

Transferability

Although written within the UK policy and practice context, the emphasis on using and critically analysing the research evidence should have some appeal to social work students and practitioners elsewhere. The confining of references to specific UK legislation to within a few pages also enhances transferability to other countries.

Recommended further reading

Some recommendations for further reading are incorporated into the text.

Learning exercises

Not included.

Outstanding features

This is a textbook that encourages the reader to consider a range of approaches to assessment, and that does not avoid dealing with the dilemmas of the contemporary practitioner.

Shortcomings

One shortcoming of this textbook is the absence of learning exercises. Another shortcoming is no mention of issues which arise when assessing clients for whom English is not their first language.

Textbook

Social work and social problems: Working towards social inclusion and social change (2000) Basingstoke: Macmillan.[76]

Authors

Gerald Smale, Graham Tuson and Daphne Statham.

Authors' affiliations at time of publication

Gerald Smale was the Director of Development at the National Institute for Social Work and Visiting Professor at Goldsmith's College, England.

Graham Tuson was Director of the Diploma in Social Work at Southampton University, England.

Daphne Statham was Director of the National Institute for Social Work, England.

Edition

First edition.

Cost

£17.99.

Intended audience

According to the back cover, this book "is essential reading for all social work students, practitioners, managers and educators".

Number of pages

255 including Bibliography, Index of Names and Index of Subjects (pp 238-55) plus Contents, List of Figures, Acknowledgements and Prologue (pp v-xiv).

Chapter titles

- Chapter 1: Introduction
- Chapter 2: Reinventing social work: key themes and tasks
- Chapter 3: Formulating the task: aid or development?
- Chapter 4: Mapping the task and processes
- Chapter 5: Social problems, social control and patterns of interaction
- Chapter 6: Managing and mapping change
- Chapter 7: Assessment and intervention
- Chapter 8: Overcoming blocks to change
- Chapter 9: Independence and marginality
- Chapter 10: Core skills: the joining skills
- Chapter 11: Core skills: the intervention skills
- Chapter 12: Epilogue.

Definition of assessment

Although assessment is not defined, the scope of the task is:

> Workers have to develop an understanding of the nature of the particular social problem being tackled, and the feasibility of different kinds of solution and their possible consequences. Realistic assessment has
>
> - to address the whole of the task;
> - to engage in ongoing negotiations with the full range of people involved in specific problems and their possible solutions;
> - to address both the change, care and social control tasks;
> - to go beyond the individualisation of social problems as the focus for assessment and intervention. (Smale et al, 2000, p 132)

Timing of assessment

For Smale et al, "assessment, intervention and service delivery are essentially the same exercise" (p 109). It is noted that in the lifespan of clients, referrals for assessment tend to arise after a change or loss.

Theoretical underpinnings

The 'Exchange Model' of assessment is proposed and contrasted with more traditional approaches to social work, referred to as the 'Questioning Model' and 'Procedural Model'.

Information obtained during the assessment process

Information obtained during the assessment process includes that obtained from and about the client, but can go far beyond this. This may include:

- hard facts, for example, the names, ages, addresses of the people involved, the relevant agencies and the legislation, policies and procedures covering their activities
- the expression of personal feelings within the networks
- the emotional response of the worker
- knowledge about a particular kind of social problem or condition
- insight into recurring patterns of relationships between people, groups and organisations
- research on models of how to bring about positive change
- information obtained from another organisation. (Smale et al, 2000, pp 224-5)

Risk assessment

Some of the content about social control would seem to be about risk management but does not use the word 'risk'.

Multidisciplinary assessment

The importance of identifying all the stakeholders in a situation is highlighted. However, the extent to which any of these are involved in conducting an assessment is unclear.

Involvement of users and carers in the process

The active involvement of service users and carers in a partnership relationship is a central tenet of the Exchange Model.

User and carer perspectives of the assessment process

Seeking to understand the experience of service users and carers is crucial.

Evidence bases

Research evidence is referred to throughout the text, and the reader is encouraged to become familiar with research that is relevant to their work.

Inclusion of case studies

Case examples are used throughout the text.

Anti-discriminatory/anti-oppressive practice

Although the terms 'anti-discriminatory practice' and 'anti-oppressive practice' are not used, the underlying philosophy of this textbook is consistent with the concept of anti-discriminatory practice.

Languages other than English and use of interpreters

The need for interpreters to have communication skills in both English and the client's language, is mentioned.

Legislation/legal frameworks

The need for social workers to work within statutory requirements is mentioned several times. Specific legislation is referred to in passing.

Accuracy

Presumably the manuscript for this textbook was prepared prior to publication of the *Framework for the assessment of children in need and their families*. There is no mention of this or any other widely used assessment frameworks. While the authors note "the Exchange Model … is unworkable if the individual is tied down by narrowly prescriptive procedures" (Smale et al, 2000, p 218), they provide no guidance as to how the model may be used in conjunction with national assessment frameworks that are often prescriptive in respect of domains that must be covered in an assessment.

Comprehensiveness

This textbook provides the reader with a way of looking at social problems, demonstrating the link between the presenting problems of individual clients and wider social issues. However, readers would need to look elsewhere for more specific content about the process of actually going about and doing an assessment.

Durability

The material in the chapters is unlikely to date rapidly. However, it is noted that the Exchange Model was advocated by the authors in a previous text (Smale et al, 1993) and thus to some extent this is an update of their previous work.

Transferability

Although written within the UK policy and practice context, the chapter on assessment would be readily accessible to social work students and practitioners elsewhere.

Recommended further reading

Not included.

Learning exercises

Not included.

Outstanding features

This textbook encourages a much more holistic approach to social work than that offered by many other textbooks. As such, it rightly identifies social problems as contributing to the referral of many individuals to social work agencies rather than attributing the source of problems to the affected individuals.

Shortcomings

Although the authors point out that "this is not a simple how-to-do-it book" (Smale et al, 2000, p 8), beginning social work students who are starting to learn about assessment would need to supplement their reading of this text with readings from other sources.

Appendix 3: Introductory textbooks reviewed and found not to have a chapter or distinct section on assessment

Adams, R., Dominelli, L. and Payne, M. (2002) *Social work: Themes, issues and critical debates*, Basingstoke: Palgrave.

Braye, S. and Preston-Shoot, M. (1995) *Empowering practice in social care*, Buckingham: Open University Press.

Davies, M. (ed) (2002) *The Blackwell companion to social work*, Oxford: Blackwell Publishing.

Healy, K. (2000) *Social work practices: Contemporary perspectives on change*, London: Sage Publications.

Lishman, J. (1994) *Communication in social work*, Basingstoke: Macmillan.

Parrott, L. (2002) *Social work and social care*, London: Routledge.

Parton, N. (1997) *Social theory, social change and social work: An introduction*, London: Routledge.

Payne, M. (1997) *Modern social work theory* (2nd edn), London: Macmillan.

Stepney, P. and Ford, D. (2000) *Social work models, methods and theories*, Lyme Regis: Russell House Publishing.

Thompson, N. (2000) *Understanding social work*, Basingstoke: Palgrave.

Appendix 4:
Assessment frameworks

Framework
Framework for the assessment of children in need and their families.

Publisher
The Stationery Office, London, on behalf of the Department of Health, Department for Education and Employment and the Home Office.

Date of publication
2000.

Related publications
There are numerous associated publications. These include:

Department of Health (2000) *Assessment of children in need and their families: Practice guidance,* London: The Stationery Office.

Department of Health (2000) *Framework for the assessment of children in need and their families: Guidance notes and glossary for referral and information record, initial assessment record and core assessment record,* London: The Stationery Office.

Department of Health (2000) *Studies informing the development of the framework for the assessment of children in need and their families,* London: The Stationery Office.

Department of Health (2003) *Assessing children's needs and circumstances: The impact of the assessment framework,* London: Department of Health.

Department of Health (2003) *What to do if you're worried a child is being abused: Children's services guidance,* London: Department of Health.

Department of Health and Cleaver, H. (2000) *Assessment recording forms*, London: The Stationery Office.

Department of Health, Cox, A. and Bentovim, A. (2000) *The family assessment pack of questionnaires and scales*, London: The Stationery Office.

Horwath, J. (ed) (2001) *The child's world: Assessing children in need*, London: Jessica Kingsley Publishers.

Intention of the framework

In the Foreword to the framework, John Hutton, the Minister of State for Social Services, writes:

> We cannot begin to improve the lives of disadvantaged and vulnerable children unless we identify their needs and understand what is happening to them in order to take appropriate action.

> The Government is committed to delivering better life chances to such children through a range of cross-cutting, inter-departmental initiatives. A key component of the Government's objectives for children's social services is the development of a framework for assessing children in need and their families, to ensure a timely response and the effective provision of services. (Department of Health et al, 2000, p vii)

While the framework has been described as providing "a systematic way of analyzing, understanding and recording what is happening to children and young people within the context of their families and the wider context of the community in which they live" (p viii), the emphasis is on more of a "conceptual map" (p 26) than a how-to-do-it guide:

> The Guidance is not a practice manual. It does not set out step-by-step procedures to be followed: rather it sets out a framework which should be adapted and used to suit individual circumstances. (Department of Health et al, 2000, p ix)

Intended audience

It is suggested that:

> The Guidance has been produced primarily for the use of profession-als and other staff who will be involved in undertaking assessments of children in need and their families under the Children Act 1989....
>
> Many agencies have contact with and responsibility for children and young people under a range of legislation. The Guidance is, therefore, also relevant to assessments concerned with the welfare of children in a number of contexts.
>
> Health, education and youth justice services, in particular, may already have had considerable involvement with some children and families prior to referral to social services departments. They will have an important contribution to make to the assessment and, where appropriate, to the provision of services to those families. (Department of Health et al, 2000, p ix)

Number of pages

109 including Appendices (pp 89-109) plus Foreword and Preface (pp vii-xii).

Definitions of assessment

The framework proposes a definition of assessment based on the work of Compton and Galaway:

> Assessment is the first stage in helping a vulnerable child and his or her family, its purpose to contribute to the understanding necessary for appropriate planning and action. Assessment has several phases which overlap and lead into planning, action and review:

- Clarification of source of referral and reason
- Acquisition of information
- Exploring facts and feelings
- Giving meaning to the situation which distinguishes the child and family's understanding and feelings from those of the professionals

- Reaching an understanding of what is happening, problems, strengths and difficulties, and the impact on the child (with the family wherever possible)
- Drawing up an analysis of the needs of the child and parenting capacity within their family and community context as a basis for formulating a plan. (Department of Health et al, 2000, p 29)

Timing of assessment

Assessment is considered to be a "continuing process, not a single event" (p 14), which is "iterative" (p 15), taking care not to "be over intrusive, repeated unnecessarily or continued without any clear purpose or outcome" (p 15). It is recognised that some situations will require more complex and lengthier assessment processes. Expected timeframes for the completion of initial assessments after referral are provided.

Theoretical underpinnings

It is noted that:

> Each professional discipline derives its knowledge from a particular theoretical base, related research findings and accumulated practice wisdom and experience. Social work practice, however, differs in that it derives its knowledge base from theory and research in many different disciplines. Practice is also based on policies laid down in legislation and government guidance. It is essential that practitioners and their managers ensure that practice and its supervision are grounded in the most up to date knowledge and that they make the best use of the resources described in the practice guidance as well as other critical materials including:

- Relevant research findings
- National and local statistical data
- National policy and practice guidance
- Social Services Inspectorate Inspection Standards
- Government and local inspection, audit and performance assessment reports
- Lessons learnt from national and local inquiries and reviews of cases of child maltreatment. (Department of Health et al, 2000, p 16)

The assessment process

Aspects of the assessment process that are outlined include:

- process of assessment and timing
- initial and core assessments
- use of assessments in family proceedings
- care applications and assessment
- disclosure
- court-sanctioned assessments
- oral evidence
- working with children and families
- planning assessment
- communicating with children
- consent and confidentiality
- assessment of children in special circumstances
- assessing the needs of young carers
- the assessment framework and children looked after
- children being placed for adoption
- children leaving care.

Information obtained during the assessment process

Three key domains, each having a number of dimensions, should be explored in an assessment:

Child's developmental needs:
- health
- education
- emotional and behavioural development
- identity
- family and social relationships
- social presentation
- self-care skills.

Parenting capacity:
- basic care
- ensuring safety
- emotional warmth
- stimulation

- guidance and boundaries
- stability.

Family and environmental factors:
- family history and functioning
- wider family
- housing
- employment
- income
- family and social integration
- community resources.

Risk assessment

Although the principles of risk assessment underpin this document, the language is of 'vulnerable children' and 'children who are suffering or likely to suffer significant harm' rather than 'risk'.

Multidisciplinary assessment

The responsibilities of a wide range of agencies and professionals are detailed in the assessment framework.

Involvement of users and carers in the process

The focus of an assessment of children should be the child, and the process child-centred, with the perspective of the child given prominence. Wherever possible, work with families should be undertaken in partnership with them:

> Generally, all these phases of the assessment process should be undertaken in partnership with the child and key family members, and with their agreement. This includes finalising the plan of action. There may be exceptions when there are concerns that a child is suffering or may be suffering significant harm. (Department of Health et al, 2000, p 53)

User and carer perspectives of the assessment process

Not included.

Evidence bases

The framework document is extensively referenced. It furthermore exhorts practitioners to adopt an evidence-based approach to their practice:

Practice is expected to be evidence-based, by which it is meant that practitioners:

- Use knowledge critically from research and practice about the needs of children and families and the outcomes of services and interventions to inform their assessment and planning;
- Record and update information systematically, distinguishing between sources of information, for example direct observation, other agency records or interviews with family members;
- Valuate continuously whether the intervention is effective in responding to the needs of an individual child and family and modifying their interventions accordingly;
- Evaluate rigorously the information, processes and outcomes from the practitioner's own interventions to develop practice wisdom. (Department of Health et al, 2000, p 16)

Inclusion of case studies

Not included.

Anti-discriminatory/anti-oppressive practice

The need for assessment practice that takes into account diversity and that addresses disadvantage and discrimination is discussed in a page on 'Inclusive practice'.

Languages other than English and use of interpreters

The use of languages other than English by both children and their parents is discussed a number of times throughout the framework, including the following guidance:

It requires sensitivity to and understanding of families and their particular needs, for example where English is not a parent's first language.... For a disabled parent, reasonable adjustments will be needed, for example, it may be necessary to provide information to a blind parent in an alternative format such as Braille or on audio tape, or to communicate with a deaf parent using British Sign Language. (Department of Health et al, 2000, p 13)

Additional specialist help may be necessary if the child's first language is not English. (Department of Health et al, 2000, p 34)

Copies of assessments and plans, in their first language, should be given to family members wherever possible. (Department of Health et al, 2000, p 42)

Legislation/legal frameworks

The Guidance describes the Assessment Framework and the Government's expectations of how it will be used. It reflects the principles contained within the United Nations Convention on the Rights of the Child, ratified by the UK government in 1991 and the Human Rights Act 1998. In addition, it takes account of relevant legislation at the time of publication, but is particularly informed by the requirements of the Children Act 1989, which provides a comprehensive framework for the care and protection of children. (Department of Health et al, 2000, p viii)

Organisational and resource issues
Two chapters, totalling 26 pages, are concerned with 'Roles and responsibilities in inter-agency assessment of children in need' and 'Organisational arrangements to support effective assessment of children in need'.

Recommended further reading
Further recommended reading is frequently referred to in the text.

Framework

A practitioner's guide to carers' assessments under the Carers and Disabled Children Act 2000.

Publisher

Department of Health, London.

Date of publication

2001.

Related publications

Department of Health (2001) *Carers and Disabled Children Act 2000. Carers and people with parental responsibility for disabled children: Policy guidance*, London: Department of Health.

Department of Health (2001) *Carers and Disabled Children Act 2000. Carers and people with parental responsibility for disabled children: Practice guidance*, London: Department of Health.

Intention of the framework

This guide is designed to be a good practice tool for practitioners carrying out carers' assessments. Children and Families assessors should make themselves aware of its contents to aid them in working jointly with their colleagues in adult services. However, it is not an alternative to the *Framework for the assessment of children in need and their families*. (Department of Health, 2001, p 1)

Intended audience

This guide is primarily aimed at staff carrying out carers' assessments of adults who are caring for adults. It is not solely for social services staff. (Department of Health, 2001, p 1)

Number of pages

28.

Definitions of assessment

Assessment per se is not defined. However, the purpose of assessments is noted as follows:

> A carers' assessment under the Carers and Disabled Children Act 2000 is carried out at the request of the carer in order:

- To determine whether the carer is eligible for support
- To determine the support needs of the carer (ie what will help the carer in their caring role and help them to maintain their own health and well-being)
- To see if those needs can be met by social or other services. (Department of Health, 2001, p 9)

Timing of assessment

Carer assessments can take place at the same time as an assessment of the person they are caring for, but can take place independently of other assessments. Assessment is not viewed as a one-off process and reviews may be required as needs change.

Theoretical underpinnings

The underpinning of this guide is the Carers and Disabled Children Act 2000.

The assessment process

Aspects of the assessment process that are outlined include:

- telling carers about carers' assessments
- timing of assessment
- assessment separately or together?
- preparing for the assessment
- one-off versus ongoing
- who should carry out the assessment?
- confidentiality and recording the assessment
- summary of assessment and the care plan/carer's plan
- content of the assessment.

Information obtained during the assessment process

A number of 'modules', each containing a series of questions about differing domains, are proposed. However, it is noted that not all modules will be relevant in all assessments, and that the questions proposed should not be considered as a questionnaire but rather a guide as to areas to explore during assessments. The modules proposed cover the following domains:

- carer's role
- breaks and social life
- physical well-being and personal safety
- relationships and mental well-being
- care of the home/s
- accommodation
- finances
- work
- education and training
- current practical and emotional support
- wider responsibilities
- future caring role
- emergencies/alternative arrangements
- access to information and advocacy
- agreed outcomes
- complaints and challenges
- review
- charging.

Risk assessment

Risk is in relation to the sustainability of the caring role, that is, whether it is at risk of breaking down.

Multidisciplinary assessment

It is acknowledged that in some assessments it will be appropriate for multidisciplinary/interagency assessments to occur.

Involvement of users and carers in the process

Carers are entitled to have their own assessment independent of any assessments of the person they are caring for. Assessments of carers should be 'carer-centred'. The practice guidance in respect of this indicates:

> The assessment is not a test for the carer. It should not be prescriptive but recognise the carers' knowledge and expertise.

> The assessment should listen to what carers are saying and offer an opportunity for private discussion so the carer can be candid.

> It should not be a bureaucratic process based on ticking boxes. It must focus on the outcomes the carer would want to see to help them in their caring role and maintain their health and well-being. (Department of Health, 2001, p 11)

User and carer perspectives of the assessment process

Not included.

Evidence bases

The reader is informed that "Research by The Social and Policy Research Unit at York University (SPRU) has identified a range of outcomes carers may see as desirable" (p 11), but other than involving discussions between researchers and carers, it is unclear how such evidence was collected.

Inclusion of case studies

A number of case studies are included.

Anti-discriminatory/anti-oppressive practice

Although the words 'anti-discriminatory' and 'anti-oppressive' practice are not specifically mentioned, mention is made of the need to ensure that carers from black and minority ethnic backgrounds are not discriminated against. One of the questions that assessors should consider in relation to sustainability of the caring role is: "How appropriate is the role for someone of the carer's culture, religion, gender?" (p 7).

Languages other than English and use of interpreters
Not mentioned.

Legislation/legal frameworks
This guidance is framed specifically in relation to the Carers and Disabled Children Act 2000. However, other legislation is mentioned, as is the *Framework for the assessment of children and need and their families.*

Organisational and resource issues
More detailed guidance is included in the associated policy guidance document.

Recommended further reading
Not provided.

Framework
Integrated care for drug users: Integration principles and practice.

An assessment framework is incorporated into this broader service framework.

Publisher
Effective Interventions Unit, Substance Misuse Division, Scottish Executive, Edinburgh.

Date of publication
2002.

Related publication
Effective Interventions Unit (2003) *Integrated care for drug users: Assessment. Digest of tools used in the assessment process and core data sets,* Edinburgh: Effective Interventions Unit, Substance Misuse Division, Scottish Executive.

Intention of the framework
The following statement is found in the framework document:

The purpose of this document is to set out for Drug Action Teams, service commissioners, managers and practitioners in the statutory and voluntary sectors

- The rationale for integrated care, its definitions and principles
- Effective practice in planning, designing and delivering integrated services
- Practical guides and tools (where possible). (Effective Interventions Unit, 2002, p 1)

Intended audience

A wide variety of services is identified as having a role in developing person-centred planning for substance users. These include:

- GPs and primary care teams
- Community-based specialist drug services
- Community and hospital pharmacies
- Scottish Prison Service (SPS)
- Providers of SPS transitional care arrangements
- Housing services
- Employment and Training providers
- Health specialties such as A&E departments, ante-natal and hepatology services
- Social Inclusion Partnership initiatives
- Social work community care, children's and family services, criminal justice social work
- Criminal Justice services such as Drug Courts, Drug Treatment and Testing Orders and Arrest Referral Schemes
- Providers of residential detoxification or rehabilitation services
- Business communities including small business forums as well as national companies and public sector employers
- Government Departments and agencies – for example education, Employment Service, Scottish Enterprise, Job Centre Plus, Progress2Work (Effective Interventions Unit, 2002, p 10)

Number of pages

160 plus Appendices, including Bibliography.

Number of pages – assessment

There are 59 pages in Chapter 4: Assessment (pp 73-121).

Definition of assessment

Assessment is defined as follows:

> The purpose of assessment is to identify the needs and aspirations of the individual in order to inform decisions about treatment, care and support for drug users. It usually takes the form of one-to-one discussions between the staff member and the individual. If the assessment process is working effectively, the individual should be a full participant and understand and agree the goals of treatment, care and support. (Effective Interventions Unit, 2002, p 73)

Timing of assessment

It is proposed that "effective assessment is an ongoing process, not a one-off event" (Effective Interventions Unit, 2002, p 73). Assessments should occur:

- At initial contact
- Regularly – but not too often
- At every transition between services
- After critical events. (Effective Interventions Unit, 2002, p 93)

Theoretical underpinnings

Single Shared Assessment, which utilises a person-centred planning approach, is advocated. These concepts are introduced to the reader and do not assume that the reader has prior familiarity with these ideas.

The assessment process

Ten pages are devoted to the assessment process. These include sections on working with individuals in a needs-led way, levels of assessment, sources of information and issues around self-reporting, assessment tools, working with other agencies, and transition from assessment to planning.

Information obtained during the assessment process

Three levels of assessment – simple, comprehensive and specialist – are proposed for use in differing circumstances. Further information about tools that can be used in these assessments is provided in a separate volume. Guidance on selecting and using assessment tools is provided.

A core data set is proposed that identifies domains of information that should be sought in the assessment process. These include:

- personal information
- drug use
- living arrangements
- physical health
- disease prevention
- mental health
- social functioning
- legal situation
- service user's perspective
- collateral information
- biological measures
- readiness to change
- risk and safety.

Risk assessment

Assessment of risk is a core aspect of assessment, both in relation to establishing access to services and priority on any waiting lists for services.

Multidisciplinary assessment

Single Shared Assessment and Integrated Care essentially involve agencies and professionals from a range of backgrounds working together to provide a coherent package of care to service users.

Involvement of users and carers in the process

The involvement of service users and carers is integral to the assessment process. Assessment should be about determining the client's needs, but should not be a process that is 'done to' people. There is a lengthy discussion of issues around the use of self-report data in the assessments of substance users.

User and carer perspectives of the assessment process

Feedback about the assessment process from a focus group of service users is included.

Evidence bases

The document is referenced throughout and, alongside each reference, the type of evidence is denoted according to the following key:

Type 1: Systematic reviews

These reviews systematically examine and appraise the level of evidence provided by well-designed primary intervention studies. These studies typically focus on one question and tend to look at the effectiveness of interventions.

Type 2: Narrative reviews

Narrative reviews look across the information provided by a number of studies but do not systematically look at the level of evidence presented. These reviews commonly address a number of related questions or issues.

Type 3: Primary research studies

Primary research studies that are relevant to the work on assessibility, assessment and planning and delivery of care are included in this type. These include randomised controlled trials (RCTs), cohort studies, cross-sectional studies, service evaluations and qualitative research projects.

Type 4: User consultations

User consultations include the series of focus groups conducted by the Scottish Drug Forum on behalf of the Effective Interventions Unit and other user surveys that have been conducted in Scotland and across the UK. These generally include data on the users' views of different aspects of treatment and care.

Type 5: EIU working groups/consultation workshops

Data collected in the course of the EIU working groups and consultation workshops that are not included in the types above. These are mostly the views of service users and commissioners. (Effective Interventions Unit, 2002, p viii)

Inclusion of case studies
There are case studies (a) demonstrating processes from a client perspective, and (b) of good agency practice.

Anti-discriminatory/anti-oppressive practice
This is not explicitly alluded to, nor is there specific mention of race and gender issues in relation to assessment.

Languages other than English and use of interpreters
Not mentioned.

Legislation/legal frameworks
There are brief mentions of legislation such as the National Care Standards for Scotland.

Organisational and resource issues
It is recognised that resources will be required for the development of core data sets.

Recommended further reading
There are numerous recommendations of additional reading, mostly with website addresses.

Framework
National service framework for older people.

An assessment framework is incorporated into this broader service framework.

Publisher
Department of Health, London.

Date of publication
2001.

Related publications
Not found.

Intention of framework

This National Service Framework is the first ever comprehensive strategy to ensure fair, high quality, integrated health and social care services for older people. It is a 10 year programme of action linking services to support independence and promote good health, specialised services for key conditions, and culture change so that all older people and their carers are always treated with respect, dignity and fairness. (Department of Health, 2001, p i)

Intended audience
Front-line health and social care staff, including social workers, community nurses, occupational therapists, physiotherapists and doctors, are among those professionals who may be involved in the assessment of older persons.

Number of pages – total
194 including Glossary, Acknowledgements, Milestone Summary and References (pp 151-94) plus Contents and Foreword (pp i-ii).

Number of pages – assessment
There are 18 pages in Standard two: Person Centred Care (pp 23-40) which are concerned with assessment. A specific 'assessment framework' is proposed within this standard (pp 34-5).

Definitions of assessment
Assessment is not defined.

Timing of assessment

The single assessment process aims to prevent duplication of assessment efforts. Front-line staff in social services, primary health or hospitals may make initial assessments at first point of contact in relation to a specific issue and refer on for specialist assessments from other disciplines.

Theoretical underpinnings

The single assessment process and person-centred planning should underpin assessment practice. These concepts are not explained.

The assessment process

Expectations as to service users and carers receiving information prior to the assessment and a copy of the care plan are outlined. It is expected that staff conducting assessments will be skilled in both multidisciplinary working and in working with older people. It is anticipated that more than one professional may be involved in a comprehensive assessment.

Information obtained during the assessment process

It is suggested that "proven assessment scales and tools should be used to carry out assessments" (p 31) but the selection of these is left with the assessor and no specific tools are recommended. The domains that should be included in a full assessment are:

- users' perspective
- clinical background
- disease prevention
- personal care and physical well-being
- senses
- mental health
- relationships
- safety
- immediate environment and resources.

Risk assessment

The role of assessments is to both identify vulnerable older adults, and promote independence where possible by seeking to prevent deterioration and manage crises.

Multidisciplinary assessment

Although a range of disciplines may be involved, the Single Shared Assessment process aims to prevent duplication of information being sought.

Involvement of users and carers in the process

Service users and their carers should be involved in decisions about care. The perspective of service users in relation to their problems and issues, and their expectations is the first of the domains listed as being required in a full assessment.

User and carer perspectives of the assessment process

Not included.

Evidence bases

The document is referenced throughout and, alongside each reference, the type of evidence is denoted according to the following key:

Evidence from research and other professional literature

A1   Systematic reviews which include at least one Randomised Controlled Trial (RCT) (eg systematic reviews from Cochrane or Centre for Reviews and Dissemination)

A2   Other systematic and high quality reviews which synthesis references

B1   Individual RCTs

B2   Individual non-randomised, experimental/intervention studies

B3   Individual well-designed non-experimental studies, controlled statistically if appropriate; includes studies using case control; longitudinal, cohort, matched pairs, or cross-sectional random sample methodologies, and well-designed qualitative studies; well-designed analytical studies including secondary analysis

C1   Descriptive and other research or evaluation not in B (eg convenience samples)

C2   Case studies and examples of good practice

D   Summary review articles and discussions of relevant literature and conference proceedings not otherwise classified

Evidence from expert opinion

P   Professional opinion based on clinical evidence, or reports of committees
U   User opinion from Older People's Reference Group or similar
C   Carer opinion from Carer's Focus Group or similar. (Department of Health, 2001, p 11)

Inclusion of case studies
Not included.

Anti-discriminatory/anti-oppressive practice
Standard One in the National framework is titled 'Rooting out age discrimination'. In relation to assessment specifically, the need to recognise individual needs, including gender, cultural and religious differences, is mentioned.

Languages other than English and use of interpreters
Languages other than English are mentioned only in relation to the provision of information:

> All information should be provided in appropriate formats. This may include providing information

- In a range of languages, depending on local needs, or as visual or spoken information, as well as the written word.
- For people with sensory impairment through languages such as the British Sign Language and the deafblind manual; and in accessible formats, for example, via large print letters, telephone, email, or textphone.
- In formats accessible to those with literacy or learning difficulties easy-read versions of leaflets using simple language and pictures. (Department of Health, 2001, p 28)

Legislation/legal frameworks
There are brief mentions of legislation.

Organisational and resource issues

The framework anticipates the development of resources such as assessment tools, and briefly discusses the organisational implications of shared assessment and interagency working for different agencies including the NHS and social services.

Recommended further reading

Nothing specifically recommended, although a lengthy bibliography is included.

Index

Other knowledge reviews available from SCIE

LEARNING AND TEACHING IN SOCIAL WORK EDUCATION: ASSESSMENT

Beth R. Crisp, Mark R. Anderson,
Joan Orme and Pam Green Lister
1 904812 00 7
November 2003

THE ADOPTION OF LOOKED AFTER CHILDREN: A SCOPING REVIEW OF RESEARCH

Alan Rushton
1 904812 01 5
November 2003

TYPES AND QUALITY OF KNOWLEDGE IN SOCIAL CARE

Ray Pawson, Annette Boaz,
Lesley Grayson, Andrew Long and
Colin Barnes
1 904812 02 3
November 2003

INNOVATIVE, TRIED AND TESTED: A REVIEW OF GOOD PRACTICE IN FOSTERING

Clive Sellick and Darren Howell
1 904812 03 1
November 2003

FOSTERING SUCCESS: AN EXPLORATION OF THE RESEARCH LITERATURE IN FOSTER CARE

Kate Wilson, Ian Sinclair, Claire Taylor,
Andrew Pithouse and Clive Sellick
1 904812 04 X
January 2004

TEACHING AND LEARNING COMMUNICATION SKILLS IN SOCIAL WORK EDUCATION

Pamela Trevithick, Sally Richards,
Gillian Ruch and Bernard Moss
with Linda Lines and Oded Manor
1 904812 12 0
May 2004

IMPROVING THE USE OF RESEARCH IN SOCIAL CARE PRACTICE

Isabel Walter, Sandra Nutley, Janie
Percy-Smith, Di McNeish and
Sarah Frost
1 904812 13 9
June 2004

TEACHING, LEARNING AND ASSESSMENT OF LAW IN SOCIAL WORK EDUCATION

Suzy Braye and Michael Preston-Shoot
with Lesley-Ann Cull, Robert Johns
and Jeremy Roche
1 904812 20 1
April 2005

Join SCIE's update list

If you are interested in a particular element of SCIE's work, or perhaps all of it, you can register your interest with us by filling out this form and posting it or faxing it back to us.

When a new publication, new information, a new event or a new commission become available we will let you know either by email or by post.

Please enter your details here

Name

Job title

Organisation

Address

Telephone   Facsimile

Email

Please tick what areas of SCIE's work you are interested in:

☐ adult services
☐ children and families services
☐ e-learning
☐ electronic Library for Social Care
☐ human resource development
☐ knowledge in social care
☐ participation
☐ social work education

SCIE commissions out much of its work. If you are interested in applying for SCIE's commissions, please tick here ☐

Data protection
The information you provide on this booking form will be held on a database so that we can keep you up-to-date with relevant publications and other SCIE news. We will not pass your details on to any other company.

Please fill out the form overleaf and return to SCIE at:

Communications Team
Social Care Institute for Excellence
Goldings House
2 Hay's Lane
London SE1 2HB

or fax it to 020 7089 6841